F 5.00

BASS GROOVES

DEVELOP YOUR GROOVE & PLAY LIKE THE PROS IN ANY STYLE

by Ed Friedland

Backbeat Books
San Francisco

Published by Backbeat Books
600 Harrison Street, San Francisco, CA 94107
www.backbeatbooks.com
email: books@musicplayer.com

An imprint of CMP Information
Publishers of *Guitar Player*, *Bass Player*, *Keyboard*, and *EQ* magazines

CMP
United Business Media

Distributed to the book trade in the US and Canada by
Publishers Group West, 1700 Fourth Street, Berkeley, CA 94710

Distributed to the music trade in the US and Canada by
Hal Leonard Publishing, P.O. Box 13819, Milwaukee, WI 53213

Cover design by Damien Castaneda and Paul Haggard
Composition by Michael Baughan
Front cover photo by Jay Blakesberg

Library of Congress Cataloging-in-Publication Data

Friedland, Ed.
Bass grooves : develop your groove & play like the pros in any style / by Ed Friedland.— 1st ed.
p. cm.
ISBN 0-87930-777-3 (alk. paper)
1. Bass guitar—Instruction and study. 2. Double bass—Instruction and study.
I. Title.

MT599.B4F94 2004
787.5'193—dc22

2004012252

Printed in the United States of America

04 05 06 07 08 5 4 3 2 1

Contents

Introduction 5
Using the CD 6
Getting a Drum Machine 6

Chapter 1: Drum Machine Basics 7
Anatomy of a Drum Beat 8

Chapter 2: Groove Concept and Development 11
Internalizing Rhythm 12
On the *One* 17
Off da Hook 19
Off da Hook, Hip-Hop Style 21
Funkin' Metronome 23
The Groove-Yard Shift 28
The Fat Factor 29

Chapter 3: The Stylistic Grooves 35
The Tramp Groove 35
The Singer-Songwriter Groove 38
The Slow 12/8 Feel 40
The Flat Tire Groove 42
The Shuffle 43
The Anticipated Backbeat 46
The James Brown Groove 48
The Bo Diddley Beat 50
Rockin' Rhumba 52
The Fats Domino 12/8 Groove 56
Slow Blues 58
Pumpin' Eighths 60
The Twist 63
The Motown Beat 66
Rock Steady 68
The Disco Octave Lick 70
Bom Bom 72
The Meters—New Orleans Funk 74
Soca 76
The Jimmy Reed Groove 80
Vinny-Boom-Batz 82
The "Green Onions" Groove 84
Cajun 86
Zydeco 90
Go-Go 92

Chapter 4: The Pros Talk Groove 97
Phil Chen 97
Harvey Brooks 98
Hutch Hutchinson 100
Victor Bailey 101
Gary Grainger 102
Jack Casady 103

Chapter 5: Groove Metaphysics 105

On the CD 109
Acknowledgments / Photo Credits 110
About the Author 111

INTRODUCTION

Playing bass is a truly universal act. The bass function exists in music of all cultures, be it American rock, Bulgarian folksong, or Caribbean junkanoo. The instrument performing the bass function may vary from one style to the next, but the essence of the bass role remains virtually unchanged—to supply the harmonic foundation (low notes, usually the root of the chord), and to create a rhythmic pulse that defines the feel of the music (groove). While the bass function also involves melodic considerations and subtleties like tone and microscopic time-flow adjustments, if you play the right low notes and you groove, you are capable of being a bass player in virtually any musical situation. Bass players who understand these core principles enjoy a degree of mobility that is unparalleled by other instrumentalists. A guitarist may be an ace country picker, but that won't necessarily help him on a metal gig. Likewise, a great metal guitarist may not have the tools to play jazz or bossa nova. But a bassist who has mastered the elements of bass function can play any style with just a few common-sense adjustments.

An important skill of the successful bassist-on-the-move is a knowledge of the rhythmic vocabularies of different styles of music. Most bass lines are constructed from the same elements—roots, 5ths, octaves, triads—with varying connecting material such as scalar and chromatic passing tones. The defining factor of a genre is most often its rhythmic content, whether it is found in the bass line or not. For example, a simple root-5 pattern in half-notes is a common bass line, but the surrounding rhythmic material can make that bass line merengue, country, samba, bossa, rock, funk, R&B, or blues. It's easy to just play your half-notes and leave it at that, but the better you understand the rhythmic material that surrounds your bass part, the better you can lock in and make it groove.

One of the goals of this book is to familiarize you with different grooves by showing you the drum parts along with the bass lines. Through the use of a drum machine, you will learn to program parts to accompany your line. It's the next best thing to being a drummer. When you've programmed a drum groove yourself, you gain an intimate understanding of each element, how hi-hat, snare, kick drum, toms, etc. all combine to create a unified feel that influences your interpretation of a bass line. Knowing how to play many different styles presents you with a greatly expanded set of opportunities. It's one of the best things about being a bass player—variety.

Keeping time is at the heart of grooving, though time and groove are not entirely the same thing—it is possible to keep perfect time and not groove, and vice versa. To keep time *and* groove is the best possible situation, of course. In the Groove Concept and Development section of this book, the exercises are designed to help you become rhythmically self -ufficient. By learning to internalize different rhythmic elements in conjunction with a non-varying time source (metronome or drum machine), you become capable of grooving from the inside out.

We bassists tend to be deep thinkers, and we have a fondness for pondering the great mysteries of life. The Groove Metaphysics chapter is more than just self-indulgent contemplation. Thinking about the groove and its many implications can open the door to your own personal rhythmic satori, that defining moment when you truly *get* what makes the groove work. All great bassists have spent time doing this, whether consciously or semiconsciously. It's part of the brother/sisterhood of the bass that binds us all together. Any bassist who has ever hit the groove and held it there has experienced the life-altering feeling of being at one with the moment. In many ways, this experience is at the heart of all religion. But I digress. . . .

Using the CD

On the CD that accompanies this book I have recorded the various grooves to help you program them for yourself. You can certainly play along with the examples on the CD, but you'll be competing with the existing bass player (me). The experience you're after is listening for guidance, then programming and playing along with your drum machine. The groove development exercises are also recorded for your convenience. Many of the exercises are easier to grasp once you've heard them.

Getting a Drum Machine

To benefit fully from this book, I suggest you purchase a drum machine. In the world of audio production the drum machine has all but been replaced by prerecorded loops of live drummers. While this approach is more realistic for crafting songs, it denies you the opportunity to create a drum part yourself. As a bassist, that experience is invaluable. Imagine having a drummer who will play exactly what you request, without slowing down or speeding up and at the right volume, plus you don't have to listen to a three-hour Neil Peart drum solo compilation on the ride home from the gig. But along with the convenience comes the task of learning what exactly to tell this magical machine. It only sounds as good as the person programming it.

There are many great-sounding inexpensive machines on the market, with companies like Boss and Zoom offering several models that cost as little as $100. These may vary in features, but they all have CD-quality drum samples and the ability to program your own patterns. Touch-sensitive drum pads are an important feature of most modern machines. Spending a little more can get you tunable drum sounds, the ability to create your own drum kits, adjustable pad sensitivity, the potential for patterns of any length and time signature, and more. These are all useful to the bassist who wants to take the drum machine to a higher musical level. But for the purposes of this book, you'll need the basics—good sounds and touch-sensitive pads. There are also software-based drum machines that work well in conjunction with a computer and MIDI controller such as a keyboard. These are worth looking into if your home practice setup is centered around your computer.

Chapter 1

Drum Machine Basics

Once you have a drum machine, read the manual to familiarize yourself with its major functions. In order to cram a lot of features into a small package, machines are designed so that many functions are accessed by combinations of buttons that are far from obvious. *Read the manual!*

While the programming architecture of different drum machines may vary, to set up a pattern you will always need to perform these basic functions:

- Select the proper pattern length. Most of the examples in this book are two-bar patterns, though there are some one-bar and four-bar patterns. Some machines represent pattern length in terms of measures—"1," "2," or "4"—while others show pattern length in terms of beats: "4" would stand for four beats, or one bar of 4/4; "8" would be eight beats, or two bars of 4/4. This type of programming architecture is useful for odd time signatures: Setting a pattern length of "5" would give you one bar of 5/4 time.

- Set the quantization level. Quantization is the degree to which the machine will auto-correct your rhythmic input. If set to 16th-notes, your input will be automatically corrected to the nearest 16th. This is very handy for a 16th-note groove, but it won't allow you to input eighth-note triplets (represented as "12th notes" by some machines). For each groove in this book I've stated the level of quantization used to program it.

- Set the record mode. Most machines let you record in either "real time" or "step time" mode. The default is typically real time; it's the method I recommend for most situations. You place the machine in record mode and play the rhythms on the specific pad in real time to the machine's internal metronome. The machine records your performance, auto-corrects anything that is off to the specified quantization level, and recycles to the beginning of the pattern when the end is reached. You can layer other drum sounds on top of the first pass as you would with a multitrack tape recorder. Step-time mode is useful if there is a tricky part that you can't manage to play in real time. Switch the machine to step mode and select the quantization level. Then forward the pattern to the correct position in the bar with a specified button, and when you reach the trouble spot, play the drum pad. The pattern will then advance automatically to the next eighth-note, 16th-note, or whatever quantization level you've set.

- Adjust the tempo. While I've listed an optimum tempo for many of the grooves, it may be necessary to play it into the machine at a slower speed. Adjusting the tempo to a comfortable speed for programming is not cheating—the real work comes when you play bass along with the pattern at the suggested tempo.

- Erase notes. You are bound to make mistakes either in reading the rhythms or playing them into the machine. That's no big deal as long as you know how to erase or delete the mistakes. Most machines have a DELETE button that you press and hold as the machine is playing the pattern in record mode while you press on the pad that corresponds to the sound you want to erase. You can either hold it for the entire pattern and reprogram the specific "instrument" sound again, or push the pad at the problem and "spot-erase" it.

- Switch pad banks. Drum machines typically have 16 pads labeled with the instrument names they trigger: "Kick," "Snare," "Closed Hi-Hat," etc. are the first layer of sounds and are the most commonly used. However, there is a second bank of pad-triggered sounds that includes instruments such as congas, shakers, tambourines, and bongos. These can be accessed by switching the pad bank. Often the names of the second bank sounds are not written on the machine, so you have to play around the pads to find what pad triggers what different sounds.

Anatomy of a Drum Beat

The drum beats in this book focus mainly on the essential groove. For now, it isn't important to learn how to program long, complex fills—most of your work will be with the kick, snare, hi-hat (open and closed), and ride cymbals. Toms will be used if they are integral to the groove, as will auxiliary percussion such as shakers, cowbells, and congas. Drum machines are capable of playing back anything you program, but keep in mind that human drummers (usually) have two arms and two legs. Remembering this will help you program realistic grooves that can actually be played by a real drummer.

The Drum Key

We're not talking about the little metal thing drummers use to tune their kit—the drum key is your roadmap for reading the drum notation throughout this book. Figure 1 shows the basic drum symbols for a standard kit. Some of the grooves later in the book may have unique percussion instruments such as congas, shakers, bells, and tambourines. That notation will be indicated next to the appropriate example.

Figure 1

Drum machine fine points

Once you have the basic operation of the drum machine under control, the real trick is to make it sound musical. Dynamics are the key. Too often people smack the pads without taking advantage of the instrument's (admittedly limited) dynamic range. Some machines, like those in the Boss DR series, have options for adjusting the pad sensitivity; this can be a great aid in developing a personal touch on the pads. While you might want to play the pads like a real drummer, you are better off playing one pad or instrument voice at a time to capture the dynamics of a part.

It's equally important to develop a consistent touch. When programming a snare backbeat you should keep the volume consistent—rising and falling volumes can mess with the groove's energy. That doesn't necessarily mean that all the backbeats should be as loud as possible. The song may require a firm backbeat, but it should be perhaps only 80% of the available level so you can reserve the remaining 20% for a big fill. The kick drum also needs a controlled touch. For the main rhythms of a groove you need a solid hit to keep it steady, but pickup notes or ghosted accents can be quieter.

Building a pattern

Let's build a two-bar pattern to practice pad dynamics. Start with a simple eighth-note closed hi-hat part. Rather than trying to get the loud/soft dynamics of the accents in one pass, start by playing just the downbeats with a firm touch (Drum Ex. 1).

Drum Ex. 1

TRACK 1

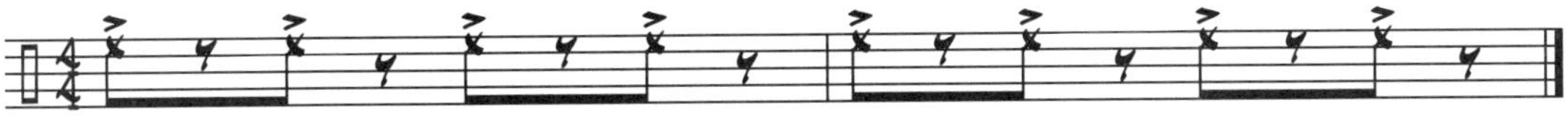

Once you're happy with the volume consistency of the downbeats, play the upbeats with a lighter touch (Drum Ex. 2). You should end up with an evenly accented pattern (Drum Ex. 3). Experiment to find the best balance between the loud and soft hits. Sometimes drummers play the upbeats almost as ghost-notes to give the groove a subtle undercurrent, and sometimes they play all the eighths the same volume for a more driving feel. Try variations to see how they effect the total drum beat and how you play bass along with it.

Drum Ex. 2

TRACK 1

Drum Ex. 3

TRACK 1

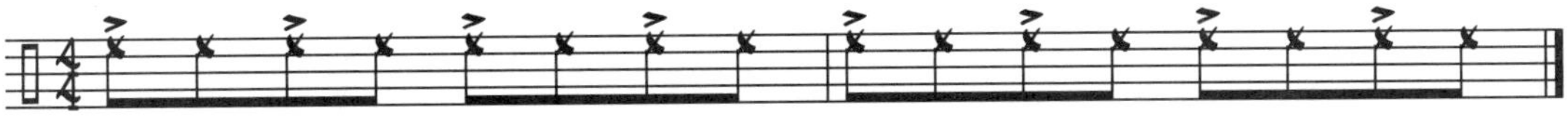

Next let's add the snare drum, a solid backbeat with a mini-fill at the end of bar 2. Play the first three snare hits at about 85% volume, the pickup on the "and" of *three* around 65%, and the last backbeat 100%.

TRACK 1

Drum Ex. 4

Now add the kick drum, playing the downbeats at around 90% and the pickups 75%.

TRACK 1

Drum Ex. 5

The complete groove will look like this (Drum Ex. 6) and should sound organic. For comparison, set up another two-bar pattern and program the same beat, but ignore the dynamics—just play everything as hard as possible. (Hmm . . . that sounds like what a lot of *human* drummers do). Compare the two versions. Which do you prefer?

TRACK 1

Drum Ex. 6

Chapter 2
Groove Concept and Development

No single phrase sums up the essence of bass playing better than "the groove." Those who have it live by it, those in need of it seek it out like the Holy Grail. But what exactly *is* groove? The word "groove" is often used to describe a rhythmic style, as in "shuffle groove" or "funk groove." Another definition is a bit more ethereal: "Groove is the energetic force created by an individual or group of musicians through the act of playing." This energy is what makes people bob their heads, tap their toes, and shake their booties. Although this definition implies the presence of a steady pulse (as in dance-oriented music), groove can also be present in forms such as classical music in which tempos may vary at the direction of a conductor. If we accept that groove is energy, then it is essentially the life force behind music. It is not bound to strict tempo, but it is most often linked to it. Time and groove are not necessarily the same thing: It is possible to keep strict metronomic time but not groove. It is also possible to rush or drag the time a bit within a tune and still groove hard. From the bassist's perspective, it's ideal when time and groove are both present. Most of our playing is within the framework of tempo, and our primary task is to create the energy of groove in real time. Developing your ability to groove is an important part of being a successful bass player—other musicians depend on you to help create this essential element.

The groove is an enigma. You can't touch it, but you can feel it. You can't see it, but you can watch its effects. It can be powerful enough to move thousands of people, but you can kill it in an instant with one stray thought. When people play together and groove, the energy is transmitted among the musicians and opens up a group link to its source. Everyone feels it, and the experience forms deep personal bonds. This energy exchange creates a euphoric state that all musicians have experienced, either as listeners or players. When that chill runs up your spine, it's the groove—the reason we play. On the other hand, when the groove isn't happening or gets sabotaged by ego or carelessness, it can turn brother against brother, create tension that will break up a band, get someone fired, ruin reputations. The groove is serious business. It is something to honor, serve, and protect. If you mess with it, you're in deep trouble.

The groove is an organic thing, like a flower (or a tomato, if you prefer). It starts with a good seed, needs fertile soil to grow in, requires nourishment and care to flourish. When it's fully grown it becomes a thing of beauty (or beautiful spaghetti sauce). While there are many active ways you can develop your groove, you can't just sit there with a metronome and become a groove monster. You also have to open yourself to the energetic force that makes the groove happen. If you try to grab water with your hands it slips through your fingers, but if you form a cup with both hands you can hold it.

Once you attain basic mechanical competence on the bass, the biggest obstacle to the groove is internal blockage. Groove is like water falling down a mountainside, taking the path of least resistance. Part of your challenge is to remove the boulders that block the flow of the groove.

Paradoxically, to achieve a state of openness to the groove, you need to consider it in its many forms. You have to examine the relationship between the kick and the bass and the kick and the snare, contemplate how the hi-hat subdivides the time, how your line interacts with all the elements of the beat, how the time flows through a song . . . but if you get too far inside your head you can paralyze your body's ability to *feel* the groove. It's a delicate balance between the mind, body, and spirit, the spirit of willingness to subvert your personal desires for the sake of the groove. Sure, you could cram a cool 16th-note-triplet fill into the last two beats of bar 32, but *should* you? Does it serve the groove, or your ego? In many ways, being a bass player is like being the guardian of the most precious element on earth, the life force. Groove makes the world go round. Would nations go to war if, instead, we could all find a way to groove together?

Internalizing Rhythm

The metaphysical dimensions notwithstanding, there are concrete, physical aspects to hitting and maintaining the groove. First, you need a minimum level of technical proficiency on your bass. You don't need killer chops—have you ever noticed that some of the strongest groove players are not the most technically oriented? Do chops ruin the groove? Hardly, but it is all too common for bassists to spend their time developing speed without considering the groove. You've seen the local hotshot at the music store furiously wanking away to the delight of slack-jawed admirers, amazing shoppers with blistering runs and other feats of pointlessness. But how many of these amp-room cowboys have what it takes to make a band rock? Make a dance floor surge? Play half-notes and make them count? You may have noticed that bassists like James Jamerson, Jaco Pastorius, Stanley Clarke, Billy Sheehan, and Victor Wooten often play a lot of notes, but that's not the point. Those players all have the groove—that's why they sound good when they let it fly. It's not about what you play, it's about how you play it.

Your ability to groove is in direct proportion to your ability to internalize rhythm, and there is no more direct route to your internal understanding of rhythm than singing. Too embarrassed to sing? Get over it—it's way more embarrassing to have a lame groove. No one cares if you have vocal pipes like Sting; for our purposes it's all about singing in the groove. Let's look at a simple syncopated eighth-note groove (Vox Examples 1–3). The accented upbeats are held in place by the rests that occur on the downbeats—just as there is no light without dark, no good without evil, there is no upbeat without downbeat. Set your metronome to 72 BPM and start feeling an eighth-note pulse. Vox Ex. 1 illustrates how to sing the eighth-notes using the syllables "da–ba–da–ba." Inhale deeply before you start; you can easily learn to sing several measures in one breath.

Vox Ex. 1

TRACK 2

After you feel locked in, start singing the syncopated rhythm, using the syllable "ch" as a place marker for the rests on beats *two*, *three*, and *four* (Vox Ex. 2). It's important to feel the space the "ch" creates—it keeps the notes in proper proportion to one another. If you cheat the rest or make it too long, you'll mess up the surrounding beats, and you can kiss the groove goodbye. Once you're comfortable with singing the groove, play it on the bass.

Vox Ex. 2

TRACK 2

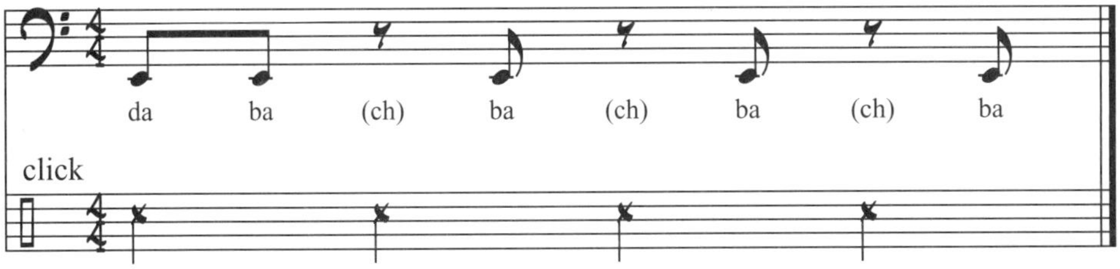

Stay with this for at least one minute—let it really settle in. Then add the notes to the groove (Vox Ex. 3). Play and sing the line together. It may be tricky at first, but it's a great way to connect your playing and your inner being. The bass is just an instrument, a tool for bringing out the groove you feel inside. If it ain't in there, it ain't comin' out!

Vox Ex. 3

TRACK 2

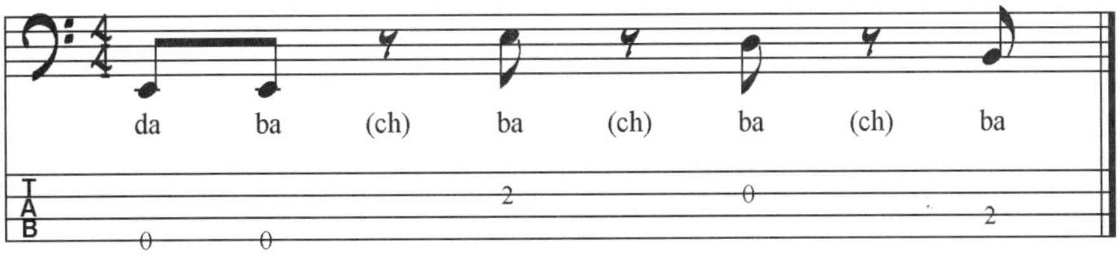

The ever-popular shuffle is one of the most frequently butchered grooves. When you play a shuffle you need to feel the eighth-note triplet undercurrent as well as the space that occurs on the second beat of each triplet group. Vox Ex. 4 shows you how to sing the shuffle's basic eighth-note triplets. Dial in 46 BPM on your metronome and fit the syllables "ba–ch–da" evenly within the space of each click, making sure that "ba" is directly on the click.

TRACK 3 **Vox Ex. 4**

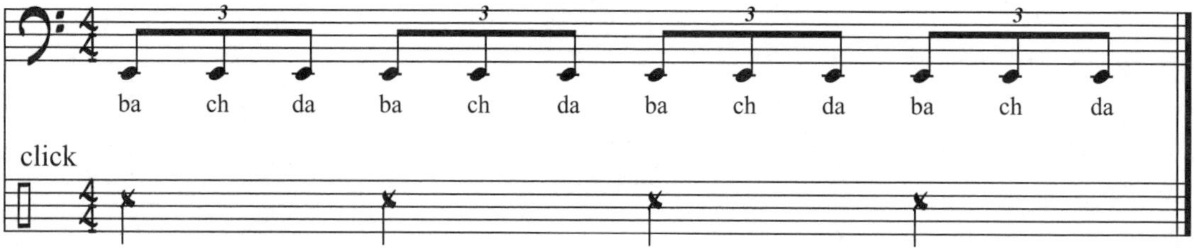

To create the shuffle groove, "ch" becomes a rest—make it quieter than the notes on "ba" and "da." Vox Ex. 5 is a classic Muddy Waters–type line. Keep the click on 46 BPM. Notice that beat *four* has a quarter-note on the downbeat, so let that note ring through the rest usually held by "ch." Sing the syllables with the pitches, and don't worry about being in tune—just make it feel good. Once you've settled in with the click, start playing the groove. When you are aligned with the flow of the rhythm, it comes to life. Notice how it feels to relax into the groove. If you internalize the rhythm of the line, you can play it perfectly, effortlessly, indefinitely.

TRACK 3 **Vox Ex. 5**

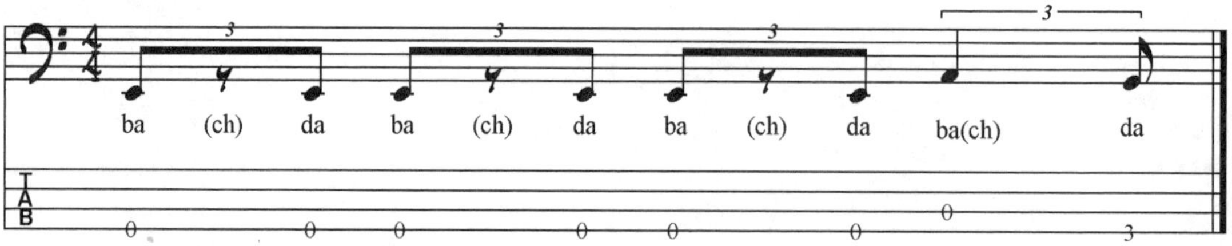

Sixteenth-note grooves can be tricky. Each quarter-note gets subdivided into four equal parts, and that's a lot of notes and space to keep track of. Traditionally, 16ths are counted with the syllables "*one*–e–and–a, *two*–e–and–a," etc., but for now we want to emphasize feel over intellect. The key to groove success is accurately internalizing the subdivisions of each beat. Vox Ex. 6 shows you a method for singing the 16th-note pulse. It's quite a mouthful, but the syllables are designed to be easy to articulate. Start practicing this around 44 BPM, making sure you nail each downbeat's first syllable ("dig") and evenly space the remaining syllables throughout the beat.

Vox Ex. 6

TRACK 4

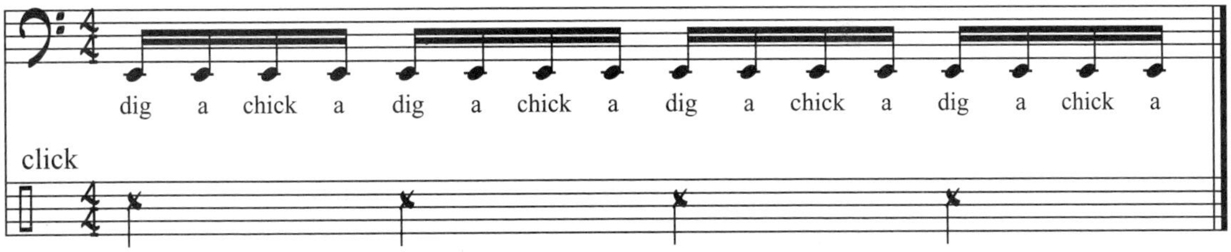

Vox Ex. 7 shows the rhythm for our 16th-note groove. Some of the consonants have been shifted to make singing them easier. Practice the syllables out of tempo at first to get the articulation, and don't forget to sing the rest on beat *four*. Once you can sing it without breaking the flow (or laughing), use the metronome at 44 BPM. Then put pitches to the rhythm (Vox Ex. 8) for the complete groove. Experiment with faster tempos—it's possible to sing this as fast as 120 BPM.

Vox Ex. 7

TRACK 4

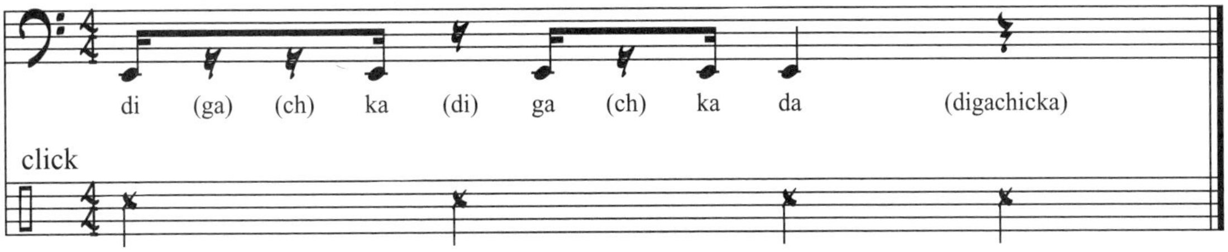

Vox Ex. 8

TRACK 4

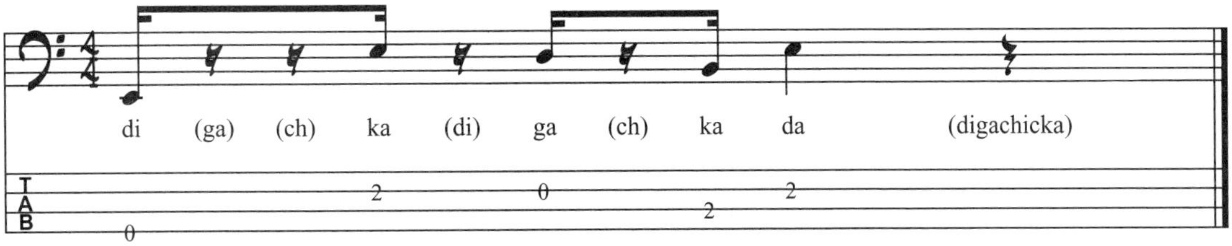

The process you've just learned can be applied to any groove. These specific syllables are just suggestions. I encourage you to find your own rhythmic language; your vocalizations will groove even harder if the language comes from you. Not only does singing rhythm help you groove, it is the best way to explain a feel to a drummer. Not every drummer will know what you mean if you tell them to play a 16th-note feel with kicks on the "a" of *one*, the "e" and "a" of *two*, and a solid downbeat on *three*. But *every* drummer will understand what you mean if you sing a rhythm to them. (Wouldn't it be nice if it were that easy to get them to understand things like "play softer" or "don't speed up"?)

So far we have looked at ways to internalize the rhythmic material contained in the bass line, but often you'll play a line that uses longer note values such as quarter-notes and half-notes. The surrounding groove may be based on 16th-notes, triplets, or eighth-notes, yet the bass line in question never uses those rhythmic values. Would you play a quarter-note line exactly the same way whether the drums were playing triplets or 16ths? Not if you want to hit the deep groove. Even if you don't actually play the beat's subdivisions, feeling them as you play your line helps you connect to the rhythmic flow. Vox Ex. 9 is a simple quarter-note line with an eighth-note undercurrent. Set the click to 80 BPM and say the syllables "da–ba, da–ba" in eighths while playing the quarter-note line.

TRACK 5 **Vox Ex. 9**

Vox Ex. 10 is the same line with a triplet subdivision, at the same tempo. Say "ba–ch–da, ba–ch–da" under the quarter-notes. Vox Ex. 11 uses the line with a 16th-note pulse, still at 80 BPM. Say "dig–a–chick–a, dig–a–chick–a" while playing the line.

TRACK 5 **Vox Ex. 10**

Vox Ex. 11

TRACK 5

For Vox Examples 9–11, on your drum machine program the kick drum on beats *one* and *three* and snare on *two* and *four*, and assign the appropriate subdivision to the hi-hat. The quarter-note subtly absorbs the "flavor" of its surroundings, with the feel shifting slightly to match the groove. This is an important fine point of hitting the big-pocket groove: Your feel needs to integrate with the surroundings.

Rhythm is a language we all intuitively understand. To prove this, pick a non-musician friend, sing a rhythm, and have the friend repeat it back to you. Most people will get it on the first or second try. If you wrote it out, it could take months before they could sing it correctly. When it comes to rhythm, hearing is understanding, and feeling is believing.

On the *One*

In the pursuit of rhythmic purity, it's sometimes necessary to strip away all the cool, shiny stuff that captures our attention and get down to the raw wood. This series of exercises pose no technical challenges; it is all about your ability to feel the tempo and groove. In their simplicity, these exercises will expose any groove weaknesses you may have. It's easy to hide behind a bunch of notes, but what happens when all you have to do is play "on the *one*"?

OTO Ex. 1 presents a simple task, yet it's amazing how many bassists can't do it right away. Set your metronome to 40 BPM and place the click on beats *two* and *four*. Tap your hand on your knee with the click, making sure you nail the beat. When your hand is in the air, starting counting: *one*, hand in the air; *two*, hand on the knee; *three*, hand in the air; *four*, hand on the knee. Use this count for all of these examples. Now, simply play your open *E* (or any note) on the downbeats (*one* and *three*), leaving the space for the click on the backbeats (*two* and *four*). Easy, right? Sure—but how accurate are you? Can't tell? Record yourself. The tape won't lie.

TRACK 6

OTO Ex. 1

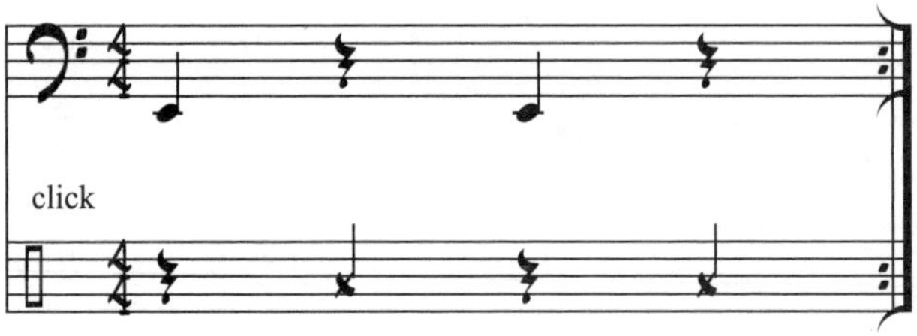

Focus on the downbeat; you need to nail it dead-on. But also pay close attention to your note lengths. Hold the quarter-note for its full value—stop the note right on the backbeat click. Imagine you have a square wooden peg that you want to fit into a groove. If the peg is the correct width, it will fit into the groove perfectly tight and not slip. But if you shave that peg by a millimeter, it will wiggle, and over time that wiggle will get bigger until the peg slips out of the groove. To create a "lock on the groove" with your bass playing, you must pay attention to your note lengths. Leaving unwanted gaps in your bass line creates slop that will eventually lead to groove breakdown.

OTO Ex. 2 requires you to play two eighth-notes on the downbeats, with the click on the backbeats. Make sure your eighths are evenly spaced and the proper length. It's important to hear the bass line and the click as one. They are not separate entities; they have to merge into one line for you to really groove. Feel the space created by the backbeat, and stay involved in the groove, even in places where you aren't playing. The rests have to groove just as hard as the notes. (It may help to internally subdivide the eighth-notes into 16ths.) For this example, imagine you're hearing Queen's "We Will Rock You."

TRACK 6

OTO Ex. 2

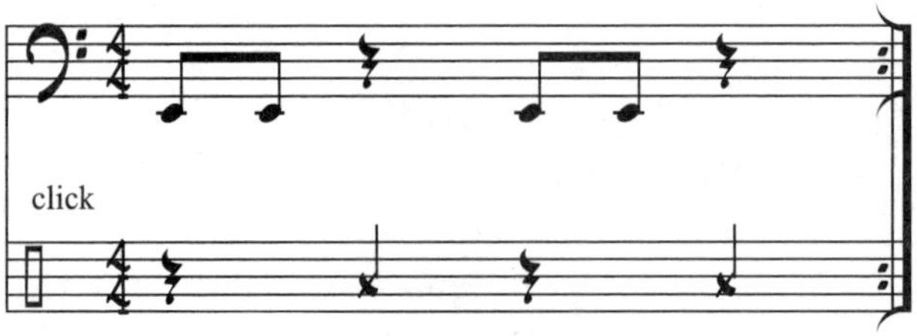

OTO Ex. 3 is a bit trickier; you're playing the shuffle rhythm, so you need to subdivide the pulse into a triplet feel. One way to get in the pocket with the triplet feel is to speak the syllables "chick–a–duh, chick–a–duh, chick–a–duh, chick–a–duh" evenly in tempo. Keep that running in your head while you play OTO Ex. 3. I suggest you practice all of these examples without tapping your foot or moving your body; the idea is to forge your internal sense of rhythm without relying on external movement. How accurate are your feet? Well, drummers have to work really hard to get their feet in sync with their hands (and many of them continue to have trouble with it). Leave your feet out of these exercises; when it's time to play your gig you can shake everything you've got.

OTO Ex. 3

TRACK 6

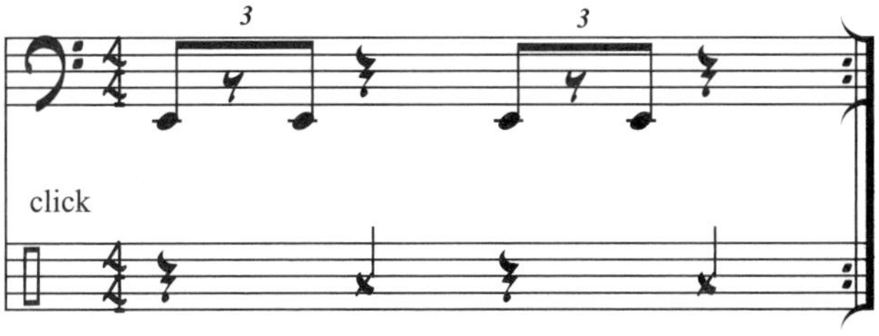

OTO Ex. 4 is trickier still. The dotted-eighth/16th rhythm is a big part of funk, rock, Latin, and other styles. To get an internal lock on the groove, say "ookachu–bop, ookachu–bop." The "ookachu" takes up the space of the dotted eighth, and the "bop" is right on the beat's last 16th (the "a" of beat *one*). Pay attention to where the "bop" falls in relation to the backbeat click. You can even say "ookachu–ba–ding," with the "ding" falling right on the backbeat click. Lining up the 16th is crucial to this groove's success. As always, listen to the space between the notes and on the backbeat, and note how they combine to create one part. Once you get comfortable with OTO Examples 3 and 4, try switching from one to the other without stopping. This requires you to internally shift from a triplet to a 16th undercurrent, which should take a chunk out of your *Road Rules* marathon viewing time!

OTO Ex. 4

TRACK 6

Your ability to feel the groove has to come from inside you. No bass, amp, drummer, drug, or member of the opposite sex will make you groove. Once you get relaxed and settled with these examples, start cranking up the tempo—you'll be amazed at the way moving up a few notches on the metronome changes things.

Off da Hook

If you've spent some time with the last batch of exercises, you'll have built a great foundation for this next series. Let's up the ante a bit and learn a similar set of exercises, this time focusing on the offbeats. To accomplish this you will need an unwavering lock on the downbeat, the ability to keep a steady pulse, and accurate subdividing skills. As with "On the *One*," use your metronome—the click will be on beats *two* and *four*. I suggest a tempo of 40 BPM; once you get solid, you can play the exercises faster.

Offbeat Ex. 1 consists of offbeat eighth-notes on the "and" of beats *one* and *three*. Since you aren't playing the downbeat, you need to keep a steady eighth-note pulse running internally.

TRACK 7

Offbeat Ex. 1

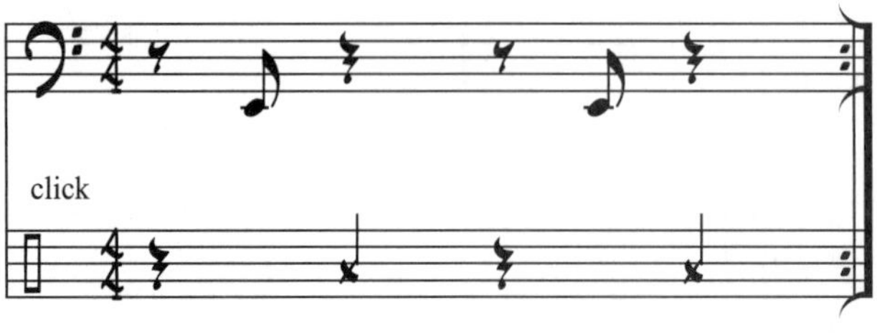

Offbeat Ex. 2 gets us grooving with the eighth-note triplet feel. Before you start, make sure you can latch onto the subdivision: Break up the triplet pulse vocally with something like "chi–ka–da, chi–ka–da" or "hi–ga–da, ba–ga–da." (Just don't get too loud if you're working this out on the bus during your morning commute.) Once you have established groove-lock, play only the second note of the triplet, or the "ka" in "chi–ka–da." Notice how the space for this beat is slightly different than in Offbeat Ex. 1. There is a subtle difference between straight eighths and triplet eighths, and there's an even subtler difference between triplet eighths and triplet 16ths. It's tricky at first, but as with all of these groove-maintenance exercises, once you're in the pocket all you have to do is let it be. When you can sense the effortlessness of nailing the groove, stop thinking and just feel it. Don't second-guess yourself, and don't mess with it!

TRACK 7

Offbeat Ex. 3 emphasizes the last note of the triplet, or the "da" in "chi-ka-da." Be sure to feel the relationship of this beat to the click on beats *two* and *four*.

Offbeat Ex. 2

Offbeat Ex. 3

Offbeat Ex. 4 takes us into 16th-note territory; for our purposes, count the pulse as "one-e-and-a, two-e-and-a," etc., and play only on the "e" of beats *one* and *three*. Offbeat Ex. 5 has you playing only the "a" of *one* and *three*.

These exercises will really tighten up your funk grooves. I can't stress the importance of this practice enough; we already know that keeping time and having a solid groove are crucial to good bass playing. If you can't lock in with these offbeats, you'll have a serious gap in your groove understanding.

Offbeat Ex. 4

Offbeat Ex. 5

TRACK 7

These examples are challenging at first; you may be tempted to give up and live in a self-created fantasy world where you're a groovemaster. But don't let this happen. The wellspring of life flows freely with the groove of eternal connectedness. Go forth, brave soldier of rhythm, and smite the scourge of the grooveless ones.

Off da Hook, Hip-Hop Style

Now let's zoom in to an even finer resolution level: 16th-note triplets. The 16th-note triplet is the underpinning for many hip-hop grooves, or the swinging funk feel us old-timers used to call "swunk."

The 16th-note triplet is the smallest subdivision unit that groove-oriented bassists need to work with. If you play classical orchestral or solo works you will face the horrors of 32nd-notes and worse. Count your lucky stars if you just want to rock!

Before you begin doing these exercises in tempo, start by tapping your feet. Keep as steady a tempo as possible until you get the feel of where these beats are located in the pulse. You can tap your right foot on *one* and *three* and your left on *two* and *four*. Once you have a feel for the rhythms, use the click and keep the tempo at 40 BPM—these rhythms are so finely syncopated you may not be able to go much faster. If 40 BPM is too fast at first, on your drum machine program a whole-note click. By setting the tempo to 80 you'll have a 20 BPM click.

Vocalize 16th-note triplet subdivisions with the syllables "hi-ga-da-ba-ga-da" to represent one quarter-note's worth. Swunk Ex. 1 shows the 16th-note triplet's pulse broken up with the syllables. Spend some time getting comfortable speaking these rhythms—after all, if you can sing it, you can play it. Find a quiet place to do this; not everyone will understand what "hi-ga-da-ba-ga-da" really means.

TRACK 8

Swunk Ex. 1

Swunk Ex. 2 emphasizes the first "ga" of "hi-ga-da-ba-ga-da," the second subdivision of the first 16th-note triplet. Swunk Ex. 3 lays into the first "da" of the same syllabic grouping. These two are very close to each other; practice them slowly and make sure you're hitting the correct subdivisions.

TRACK 8

Swunk Ex. 2

TRACK 8

Swunk Ex. 3

Swunk Ex. 4 accents the grouping's second "ga" (from the "ba-ga-da" half of the pulse). Finally, Swunk Ex. 5 works the second "da," the last subdivision of the second triplet. This one is tricky to nail because the 16th-notes are so close to the clicks on *two* and *four*.

TRACK 8

Swunk Ex. 4

TRACK 8

Swunk Ex. 5

I hope you will face the dragon and master these exercises. They will make you more aware of the various levels of rhythmic activity that exist in the grooves we play. Practicing them will make you a much stronger player in a way that has nothing to do with your chops. As you've noticed, it doesn't take technique to nail these exercises; it takes feel and patience—two very important qualities for a successful life as a bass player.

Funkin' Metronome

Everyone loves to slap. It's fun, flashy, and a great way to amaze your family and impress your friends, and in some instances it's actually the most appropriate thing to do musically. Assuming that you already have the basic technique together, the question is—are you grooving? Slapping involves a very different mechanism than fingerstyle playing, and even if your groove is generally good with the fingers, it's important to do time/groove work with your slap style. Due to the highly kinetic nature of slap, it's common for players to succumb to *Momentum Acceleritis.* Like a boulder picking up speed as it rolls downhill, flattening everything in its path, the *MA*-inflicted slapper destroys the groove by pushing the tempo faster and faster until no one can keep up. ("*Momentum Acceleritis* is a crippling disease affecting thousands of bands every year. Won't you help?")

The best way to gauge your time and groove is to slap along with a metronome. (You can program a straight quarter-note click in your drum machine.) If you can't keep it locked in with a click, you have a problem. Many people think practicing with a metronome will prevent them from developing their own feel, that their playing will become sterile and motorized. I understand this concern. However, once you turn off that metronome, you're on your own. Sink or swim, *your* groove is going to come out, so why not spend some time developing time? It's possible that you rush and don't even know it. The metronome will never lie to you—but you may not like what it says. Part of making the commitment to becoming a better musician is choosing to face down your weaknesses, whatever they may be. The good news is, it's actually fun to work on slap with a metronome. When everything locks in, and you're hitting the groove, it feels effortless.

Through focused use of the metronome, you can learn to keep time and to groove for yourself. The key is to vary how you use it. Simply using the metronome as a quarter-note source isn't enough. You need to vary the tempo and shift the click around to different beats. Slap Ex. 1 is a cool line that isn't too hard to play. It does have some syncopation, but it lays comfortably on the neck. The first step is to slowly master the line and get all the technical moves into your hands—the better you know the material the more relaxed your groove will be. Try to develop a rhythmic sentence for this line so you can sing it. Now add the metronome, clicking quarter-notes at a moderate tempo, like 72 BPM—not too fast, not too slow. Pay attention to how the eighth-notes align with the click, and make sure the 16ths in bar 2 stay locked in—don't rush them.

Commit to playing the example for at least three minutes without stopping. That doesn't sound like a long time, but you'll be surprised how tempting it will be to stop after 40 seconds. You may think to yourself, Hey, I've got this down, time to move on, but how you play a groove can change over time. It's important to learn to stay focused.

If you're playing a gig and the dance floor is full, you'll be playing that groove for a long time, so you need to stay loose, relaxed, and in the pocket. Take notice of the mind's tendency to wander after a minute or so. That's natural, but you can learn to prevent it by forcing yourself to play this lick for three minutes without stopping or changing it. If you get off track, start over until you've completed the three minutes. By gradually increasing the duration, you'll learn valuable lessons about staying in the moment and about how a groove can deepen over time.

TRACK 9

Slap Ex. 1

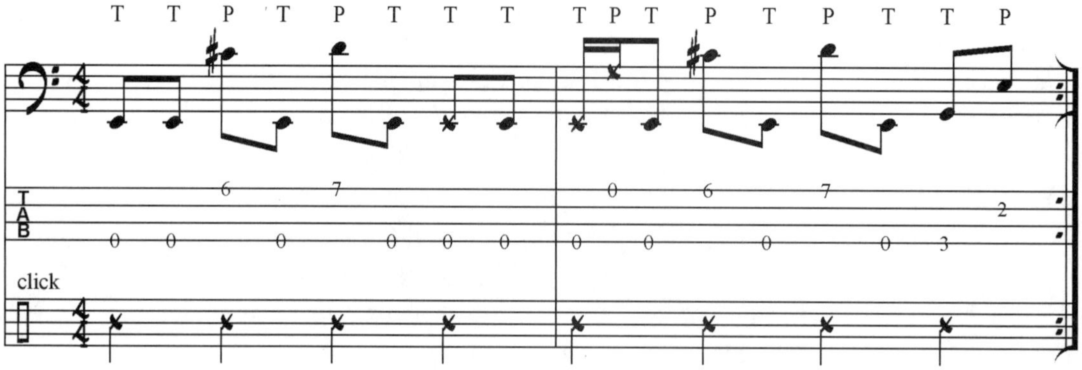

Once you get comfortable with this tempo, slow it down, perhaps to 50 BPM. You'll be amazed how different it feels. You'll need to completely readjust your sense of where the groove is, and, most important, shift the mechanism—you may have developed muscle memory for the original tempo, causing you to try to creep back up to 72 BPM. With a live drummer, this translates to groove friction—you'll be pushing against the feel, and eventually the tune will either speed up or you'll get a drumstick thrown at your head.

Next, slow down all the way to 40 BPM, much slower than you might ever want to play this lick. Though it's not an ideal tempo for a groove like this, you must be able to make it feel good at *any* tempo. It's all about the control: The tempo is what it is, not what you'd like it to be, so just accept and commit to it. You'll need to sing this, get it into your body, subdivide 16th-notes internally, chant your favorite mantra, or whatever it takes to make it happen. Don't forget—three minutes minimum!

Now that you've tortured yourself in the low tempo range, kick it up to 100 BPM. That's a much better tempo for this line—it will feel good immediately. You may notice how the time spent at 40 BPM has given you a very solid sense of where this groove is. Continue working on this example at higher speeds. It gets a little silly past 160 BPM, but it's also important to learn how to relax at fast tempos. Remember—three minutes. If you can't hold it that long, do it slower and build up. Your groove stamina is a direct product of your ability to relax.

Slap Ex. 2 cuts the click in half, placing it on beats *one* and *three*. Starting out at 40 BPM with this type of click is actually playing the line at quarter-note equals 80 BPM.

Starting at a comfortable tempo, you'll notice how the click leaves you more responsible for keeping the groove. It's not there to hold your hand every quarter-note, so don't freak out and start rushing. Listen for how the click matches up with the line and be aware of exactly what note you're playing when it hits. The effective tempo range for Slap Examples 2 and 3 is 40 to 80 BPM.

Slap Ex. 2

TRACK 9

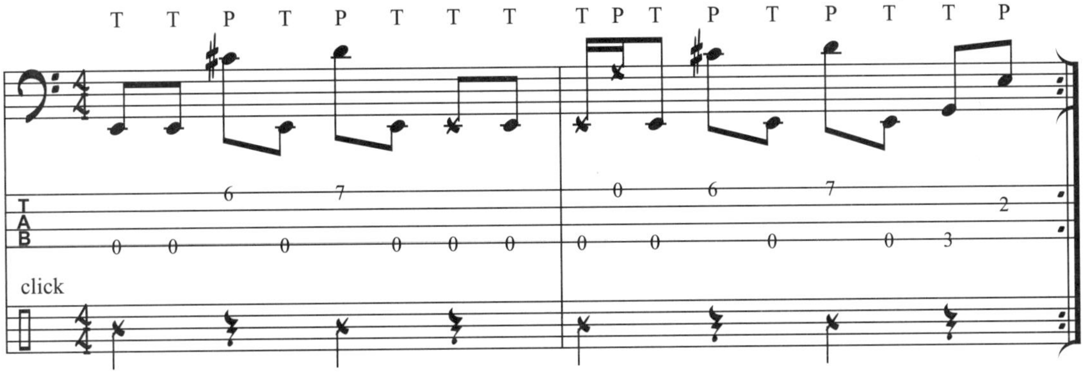

Slap Ex. 3 uses the most important method for developing your groove: placing the click on beats *two* and *four*. Virtually all grooves in popular music place the *two/four* backbeat on the snare drum. Rock, blues, funk, country, polka—you name it, the snare is slamming on *two* and *four*. Practicing this way keeps you responsible for the downbeat (look in your Official Bass Player's Job Description Handbook; that's item No. 1!), and this kind of practice trains you to lock in with the backbeat. Once again, start at 40 BPM. If you can't shift the click over to *two* and *four*, try this: Slap your hand on your knee with the click. When your hand comes up in the air for the next slap, start counting *one*; when you slap your knee, that's *two*; hand up is *three*; slap is *four*. Spend some time feeling the tempo this way before you start playing. Notice where the click falls in the line; make sure you're dead-on with it and that everything between the clicks is even

Slap Ex. 3

TRACK 9

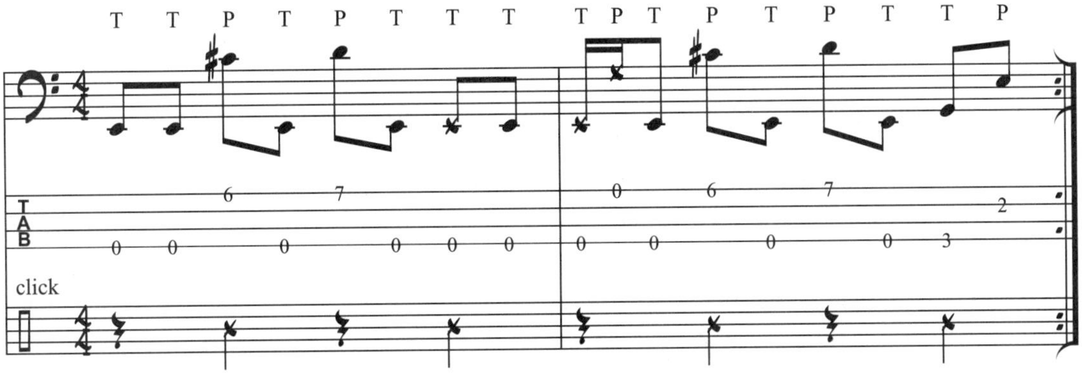

and relaxed. After you've spent time at 40 BPM (three minutes at least), start cranking up the tempo. So far we've been choosing tempos in the slow, medium, and fast ranges, but another important process is to work with many different tempos in the same range. You'll be surprised at how different a groove can feel when you change the tempo just a few BPM. People tend to develop a feel for certain tempos and subconsciously try to nudge any tune they play to a favored slot. Avoid this by becoming comfortable at any tempo.

The next series of examples takes the click even further out of the picture. One click per measure means it's going to be fast, even at 40 BPM. Depending on what drum machine you use, you may be able to set your tempo as low as 20 BPM. If your machine bottoms out at 40, then program the click on beats *one* and *three* of the pattern. This half-note click will play at half the speed, so setting it to 60 BPM will actually give you 30 if you count the click as a quarter-note. Dropping into the sub-40 BPM range is a double-edged sword: Playing the example becomes technically easier, but due to the longer space between each click, it becomes a bigger challenge to stay locked in. Either way, you'll get a great groove workout.

Slap Ex. 4 has the click just on *one*, so make sure you can accurately feel the tempo before you start. It's a real challenge to keep the pattern even and relaxed at this tempo, but it's possible.

TRACK 9

Slap Ex. 4

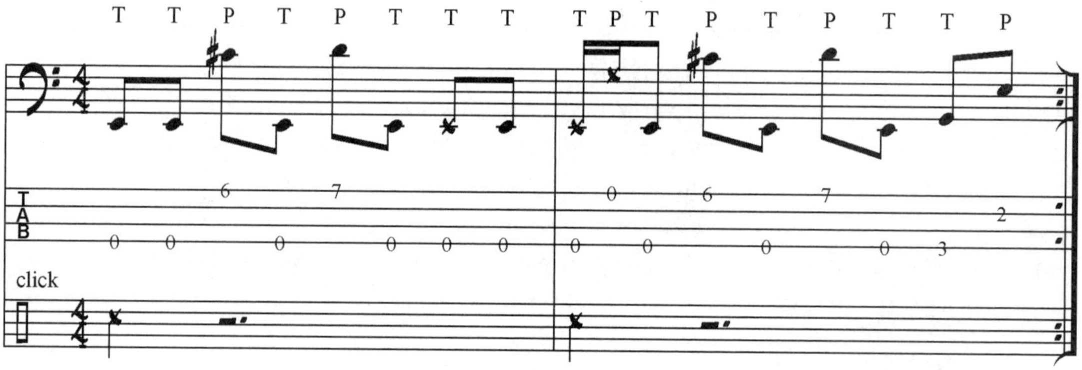

Slap Ex. 5 puts the click on *two*. It's tricky at first to get the count, but this will help: Start counting on the click, *two, three, four, one, two, three, four*, etc. Get steady with the pulse, and then emphasize *one* to make that feel like the downbeat, like this: *two, three, four, ONE, two, three, four, ONE, two, three, four*, etc. Count this way until you feel completely in sync with the beat pattern, and then start playing. The trick is to keep *one* feeling like the downbeat, even though there is a tendency to make the click feel like *one* even if it's on another beat.

Slap Ex. 6 puts the click on *three*. Use the same process for getting the click positioned: Start counting *three, four, one, two, three, four, ONE, two, three, four, ONE, two, three, four*, etc. This will feel fairly natural, since *three* creates a half-time backbeat.

Slap Ex. 5

TRACK 9

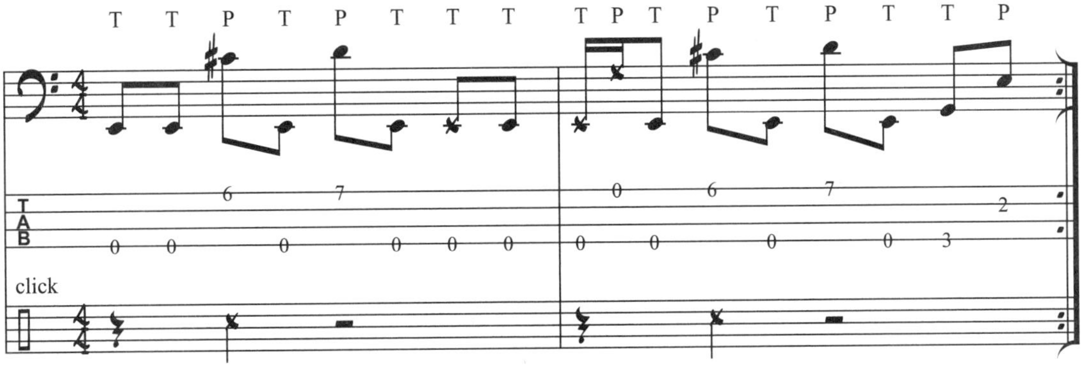

Slap Ex. 6

TRACK 9

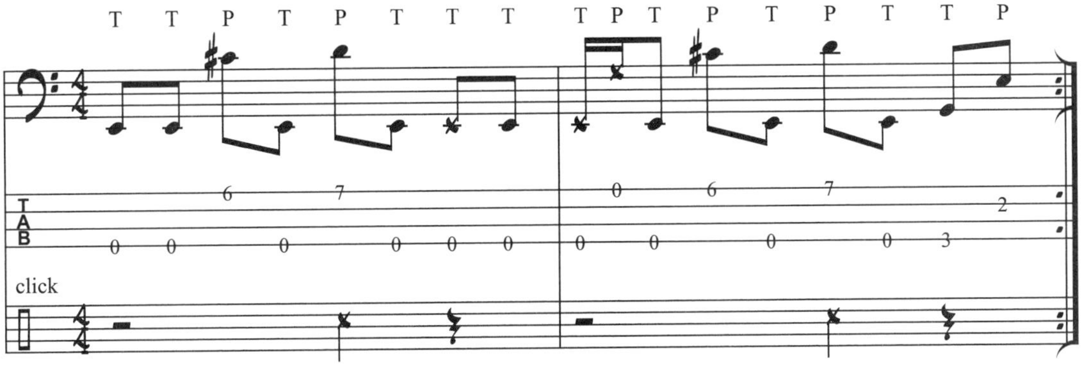

The last of this series, Slap Ex. 7 puts the click on *four*. Use the same method as before for getting into the count, or try this: Listen to the tempo and feel the quarter-note pulse, and start your count after the click: click, *ONE*, *two*, *three*, *four*, *ONE*, *two*, *three*, *four*, etc. Make sure you're steady with the count before you play, then jump in and groove for at least three minutes.

Slap Ex. 7

TRACK 9

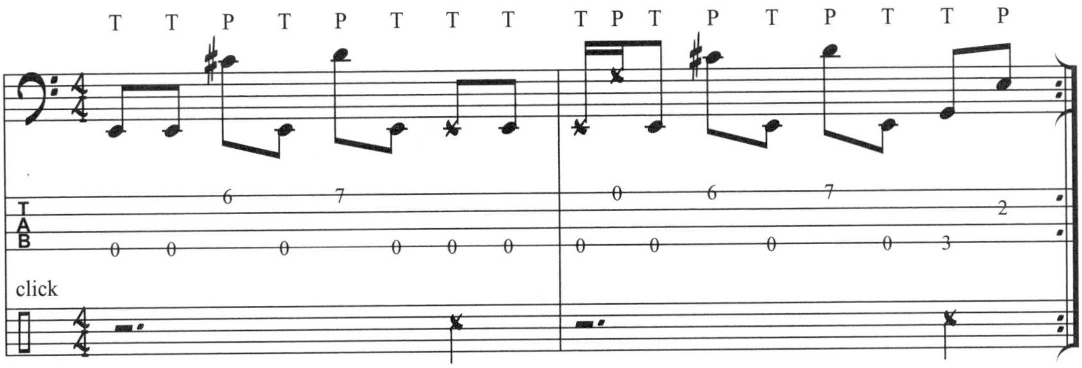

This entire process can be adapted to any 4/4 bass line, in any style. Slap has its own set of mechanical challenges, as do fingerstyle and pickstyle. If you play in a band, use this process to work out some of the bass lines from your set—it will be an ear-opening experience.

The Groove-Yard Shift

By now you understand the importance of internalizing the subdivisions of a groove. We've already looked at the difference between straight rhythms and swing rhythms, and most of the time a tune will be one or the other—the subdivisions will stay the same. However, it's possible for a tune to switch from straight eighths to swing eighths, especially in jazz. Whether or not you run into this situation, the ability to internally shift from straight eighths to swing eighths is a valuable skill—and it's quite a challenge at first.

Shift Ex. 1 is a basic R&B groove with syncopated rhythms. It's shown with a straight-eighth drum beat underneath. Play it for a few minutes to get comfortable; 90 BPM is a good tempo to start with. Shift Ex. 2 is the same lick, but written in triple meter to create the swing feel. Underneath is essentially the same drum part, except the hi-hat is

TRACK 10

Shift Ex. 1

TRACK 10

Shift Ex. 2

quantized to eighth-note triplets (or 12th-notes, depending on your machine). Play the line with the swing feel for a few minutes.

It's easy to hear how similar these two examples are, yet each is unique. The trick is learning to switch from one to the other. Shift Ex. 3 does just that: two bars of straight eighths into two bars of swing eighths. Set up a four-bar pattern on your drum machine: With the quantization on eighth-notes, program the kick and snare for all four bars and the hi-hat for just the first two. Once this is set, switch the quantization level to eighth-note triplets and program the last two bars of hi-hat.

TRACK 10

Shift Ex. 3

With this hybrid drum pattern you can now practice making the "groove-yard shift." Set the tempo to 90 BPM and listen to the drum beat closely. The tempo doesn't change, but the feel changes radically in bar 3. Now it's up to you to play the line and make the shift happen. When you get the hang of it, it's fun to switch gears like this, and it teaches valuable lessons about the physical nature of each feel. If you want to take this a step further, program a two-bar pattern with only one bar of each feel. Even crazier is a one-bar pattern that switches on beat *three.* And if you really want to take care of business, skip the drum beat and use a quarter-note click—it's now completely up to you to make the shift happen!

The Fat Factor

An important element of the groove is your notes' "dimension": their length and density. While there is no standardized system of measurement to gauge this, there are several "dimensions" that contribute to the size and weight of a note.

Note length

By now it's apparent that where you start your note has a big impact on the groove, but less obvious is the effect of note length. Where you *stop* the note is just as critical to the overall feel. Optimum note length depends on several factors: Tempo, the level of rhythmic activity, the amount of "bass energy" (more on that soon), and stylistic esthetics all contribute to defining effective note length.

When you sound a bass note, it fills a very large space in the sonic spectrum. When that note stops, it leaves a hole that can be perceived as "negative rhythm." You essentially create a rest when you stop a note, and the placement of that rest can alter the groove. Random and/or indiscriminate note lengths wreak havoc on a groove. Fat Ex. 1 is the classic "singer-songwriter" groove. Shown in the long version—in which the dotted quarter is held full length—it works great for slow and medium tempos to create a relaxed, flowing feel. Fat Ex. 2 is the short version in which a rest is placed on *two* and *four*. This tightens up the groove by leaving a nice big hole for the snare drum to live in.

TRACK 11

Fat Ex. 1

TRACK 11

Fat Ex. 2

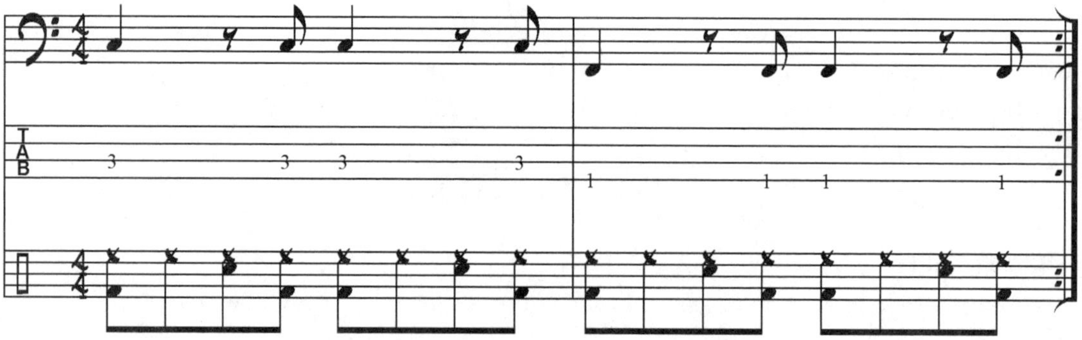

Fat Ex. 3 is a mess! Played literally, the variations in note length never let the feel settle, and the groove loses any sense of consistency and structural integrity. Unfortunately, many people play it this way without realizing it.

Fat Ex. 3

TRACK 11

In addition to keeping the feel consistent, proper note length makes your bass part lock in with the rest of the band. Remember, your bass line is the foundation of the entire band—everything you do has a profound effect on the music.

Density

A note's density is largely determined by how much bass energy it has. For example, play an *A* on the 2nd fret of the *G* string. The note will have a clear, singing quality: The physical characteristics of playing that note on a long length of thin-gauge string makes it so. Now play *A* on the 7th fret, *D* string. This note has a warmer, fuller quality, but it still retains its sweetness. Because it has more bass energy, it will carry more weight in a groove. Play *A* on the 12th fret, *A* string; you'll hear a totally different characteristic. The note is much darker in tone and has quite a bit of "oomph" to it, and it sounds perhaps less "pretty." This choice has a lot of bass energy and will work well in situations where you really need to push the band and make it sound full. For a real shock, play *A* on the 17th fret, *E* string. This *A* carries the most weight due to the short, fat length of string that's creating it. It's not a particularly sweet-sounding note. There may be audible overtones, and, depending on how your bass is set up, it may be slightly out of tune. Still, that note could come in handy in certain situations. Muted with your palm or your left hand, it could have the impact of a small bomb. Being aware of its properties will allow you to use it wisely.

Understanding your instrument's inherent qualities will guide you to the best choices for any given musical situation. Would you deliberately choose to play the biggest, fattest *A* during a quiet, laid-back section of a tune? Let's hope not. Or would you play the 2nd fret, *G*-string *A* to drive the band in the midst of a full-out heavy rock tune? Not if you want to sound appropriate. These factors definitely effect the groove. Fat Ex. 4 sets up a basic eighth-note rock feel using the different *A* notes you've explored. Play each one for a while to get a sense of how they react. Try changing the tempo to see how that changes things, as well.

TRACK 11

Fat Ex. 4

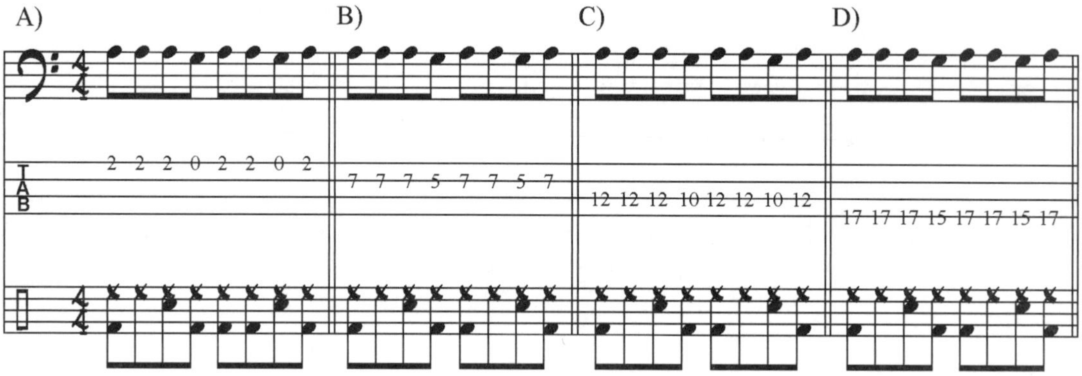

Speed-to-weight ratio

The heavier a note, the slower it needs to be played. Big, dense bass notes don't function well at fast tempos. Imagine trying to juggle bowling balls—not much fun. But juggling softballs is quite workable (assuming you know how to juggle). Notes can be weighted in terms of their rhythmic values—whole-notes being the heaviest, 16th-notes the lightest. Of course, tempo plays a role, too; a 16th-note at 40 BPM is equivalent to a quarter-note at 160 BPM. To play a 16th-note groove you need to slim down the note so it can speak. A fat, heavy note takes up a lot of room in the sonic spectrum—it won't register with the ear unless it gets the proper space. Playing fat notes too fast sounds like a drunken tap-dancing elephant. Is that the feel you want to create? (Granted, there may be a time and place for drunken tap-dancing elephants, but they should be employed with caution.)

There are several ways to work with note density. As we've just discussed, fingerboard placement is helpful. Play the lick in Fat Ex. 5 in the four different positions shown. Which sounds best? The first two give you nice note clarity, the third one starts to get a little big, and the last is probably best left alone.

TRACK 11

Fat Ex. 5

Another factor affecting note density is placement of your right (plucking) hand. Plucking a string closer to the bridge thins out a note and gives it a firm attack. The string tension at the bridge limits the amount of string movement, or excursion, producing a thinner-sounding note. Playing at the bridge also allows the string to snap back into place faster after being plucked, making quick 16th-note lines easier to play. This technique was made popular by Jaco Pastorius. Playing close to the bridge and using the bridge-position pickup on his Fender Jazz Bass, he executed amazingly fast lines and grooves that spoke clearly. Of course, this was not the only technique he used, but when it was time to play that type of line, his right hand was in the bridge position.

Moving the hand closer to the neck, the next common resting spot is over the pickup closest to the neck (on a two-pickup instrument) or over the only pickup (on a Fender Precision–style instrument). When you play in this position on a one-pickup Ernie Ball/Music Man Stingray–style bass, you have to rest your thumb on the face of the instrument.

This middle playing position works for most everything, giving you a nice balance of punch, weight, and clarity. Still, as the tempo climbs, you may find that 16ths will not speak as clearly when played there.

The last right-hand zone is next to the fingerboard—you can rest your thumb on the end of the board and play directly in front of the last fret. It's possible to play even farther up the neck. The tone gets rounder and a bit hollow, but it works great for walking bass lines or ballads—I don't suggest playing Tower of Power–style funk that way. This position creates the greatest amount of string excursion; on a fast 16th-note line the string won't snap back into place in time for you to play your next note.

Let's experiment. Fat Ex. 6 uses the line from the previous example. This time, play it using the three different areas of right-hand placement to see how the tone and weight of the note changes. The feel of the string will greatly affect how you play the line. Once you've spent some time with each right-hand placement, play the notes of this line in the four different neck locations. By altering your right-hand placement you can expand your possibilities greatly—even the highest neck position will work if you pluck the string near the bridge. Remember, these right-hand zones are just three points on the

Fat Ex. 6

TRACK 11

R.H. Bridge Position | R.H. Front Pickup Position | R.H. Fingerboard Position

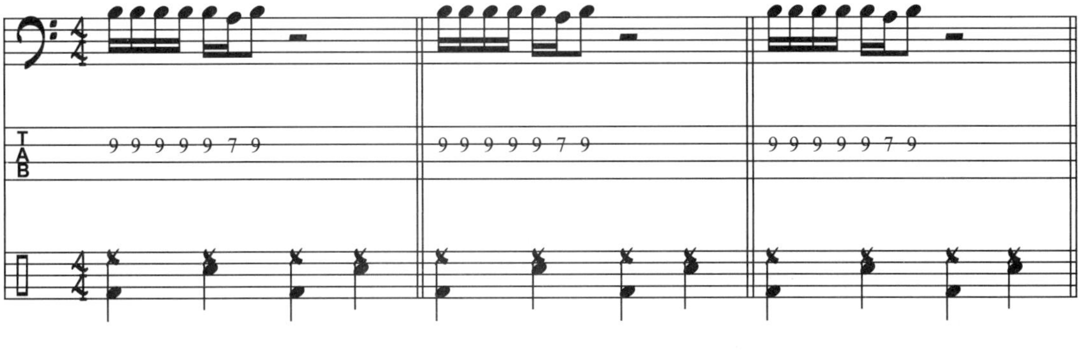

string; you can achieve a wide range of tonal variation by experimenting along the entire string length.

This concept works in reverse. If you need to play big, round whole- and half-notes, it's time to get into the Fat Zone. Fat Ex. 7 is a laid-back line that wants to be played full. I've placed it in four different areas of the neck. Start with the right hand in the middle position (over the front pickup), and see which area gives you the optimal note weight.

TRACK 11

Fat Ex. 7

Now that you understand how a note's density can significantly change the feel of a bass line, it's up to you to determine what works best for any particular moment and to know how to achieve the desired result. Stylistic considerations are important in hitting the groove; for example, playing a blues shuffle using a thin bridge-pickup tone sounds wrong, no matter how good your note placement and length is. Listening to different types of music is your best educational source. For any given style, listen to the tone of the bass, the density of the notes, and the note length. Those are all important to nailing the feel. While it's cool to experiment with cross-pollination and create hybrid feels, the secret to a successful bass career is knowing how to cop authentic grooves for many different types of music. When you get in a band that wants to be creative with stylistic combinations, let your imagination run wild. But to keep your telephone ringing, play the right feel.

Chapter 3

The Stylistic Grooves

Time for a little reality check. Do you groove? Do you effortlessly lock in with whatever tune is being played? Do you know how to lay down the perfect line for any style, regardless of whether you've played the song before? Can you subjugate your ego and chops to serve the music? Are you willing to play the line, the whole line, and nothing but the line?

Having chops is great, being musically aware is very helpful, and having the best gear makes you (and manufacturers) happy. But if you ain't groovin', you ain't worth an old, corroded, chewed-up *D* string. Let's deal with this issue now before you get out on the scene and start annoying people. If you've been playing awhile, you will still want to pay attention. After all, your groove can never be too good—and you may find it's not as strong as it could be.

The Tramp Groove

In this chapter we'll look at different musical styles and break down the groove elements, examining what we play and how it interacts with the whole tune. Tramp Ex. 1 is a basic R&B groove known as the "Tramp" groove for the Otis Redding/Carla Thomas tune that featured it. This bass line has graced countless records and thousands of bandstands, and fueled many a long-winded sax solo. Let's first start with a simple click. Set the metronome to 80 BPM and play the line. Make sure to "play" the rest—cutting off the quarter-note on beat *two* creates the right note length to make it groove, and also allows room for the snare drum that would fall there. How does it feel? Are you rushing the eighth-notes? Maybe you're getting a little behind the beat because it's a bit too fast for you. Or perhaps you can nail it perfectly—good for you!

Tramp Ex. 1

TRACK 12

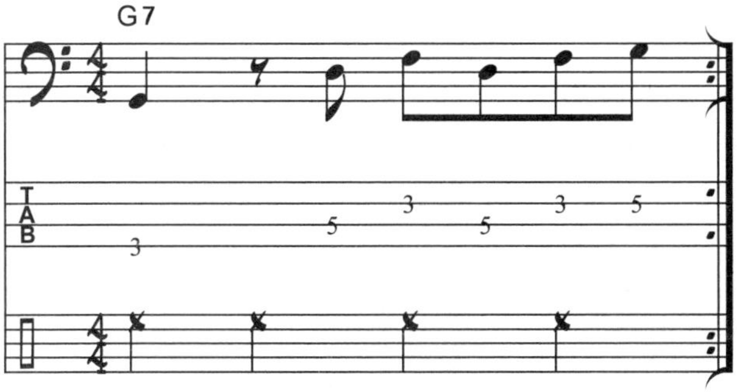

Now turn down your metronome to 40 BPM. Play the line again. At this tempo, note length becomes even more crucial, so let the quarter-note ring for its full length. It seems ridiculous to play the line at this speed, doesn't it? "No one will ever do this groove at this tempo," you say. "Why should I bother practicing it?" The main reason is that you *must* be able to do it, since time and groove are not tempo-specific. No matter what tempo is called, that's where you have to make the song groove. Put the click up to 120 BPM and play the line again. Now how does it feel? Do the eighth-notes feel relaxed? Crank it up to 160 BPM. Still able to relax? Tap your foot only on beats *one* and *three* and see if that helps you lock in. Copping the groove is more about being able to relax with a tempo than it is about your chops.

TRACK 12

For Tramp Ex. 2, put the metronome back down to 40 BPM and count the click as beats *two* and *four*. This leaves more open space and makes you responsible for the downbeat. Listen to how the quarter-note on *one* cuts off right on the click.

Tramp Ex. 2

Tramp Ex. 3

For the next four examples use your drum machine—let's see how the Tramp bass line feels with different drum patterns. The key is to notice how the subdivisions in the drum part affect what you play. Pay attention to the subtle accent shifts that happen when you lock in with different feels. Tramp Ex. 3 is the simplest groove; the drums play straight quarter-notes on the hi-hat, *one* and *three* on the kick, and *two* and *four* on the snare. Your part is the only one playing eighth-notes—how does it feel? Can you keep your eighth-notes steady?

Tramp Ex. 4 is the same except the hi-hat plays eighth-notes, so you have to match the hi-hat. Is this easy to do at a range of tempos? The kick drum reinforces your part with the eighth-note on the "and" of *two* and *four*.

Tramp Ex. 5 has a swingy, hip-hop feel. It's different to play the line with this subdivision happening, so you need to adjust your eighth-notes and make them looser—not really a shuffle, but with less of a straight-up-and-down feeling. Quantize the hi-hat to 16th-note triplets (or 24th-notes).

TRACK 12

Tramp Ex. 4

Tramp Ex. 5

Tramp Ex. 6 is a straight-16th feel against your eighth-note groove. Does the hi-hat make you feel on edge? Can you relax your line and make it fat, even though the drum part is subdividing the beat so much?

The last variation is often called the "Shotgun" groove, after the Junior Walker hit of the same name. It was also used on the '80s Hall & Oates hit "I Can't Go for That (No Can Do)." Make the first eighth-note of beat *two* nice and short; the groove needs a little space before it starts to move off the "and" of *two*. Experiment with playing the last four eighths short, too. Use a half-open hi-hat to get that old-time R&B feel.

Notice how all these different drum beats change your interpretation of the line. It's this level of detail that makes the difference between being in the pocket and not. Work out these variations at many tempos—slow, fast, and half-fast. Pay attention, and keep it grooving.

TRACK 12

Tramp Ex. 6

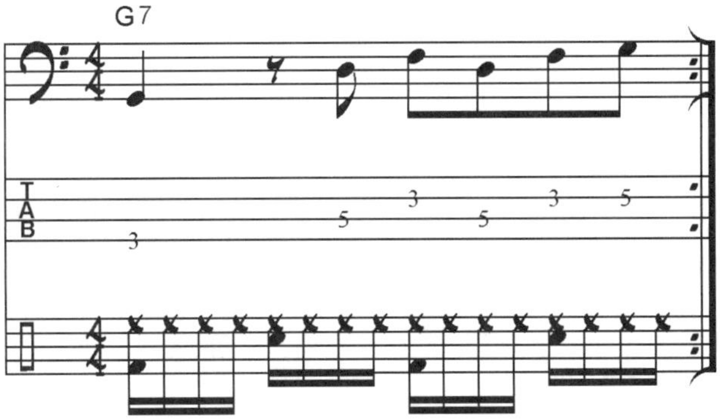

Tramp Ex. 7

The Singer–Songwriter Groove

Let's look at a classic groove: the ubiquitous dotted-quarter/eighth-note pattern sometimes called the "singer-songwriter groove." This rhythm has many applications in folk, rock, pop, country, Latin, soul—you name it. Its performance varies slightly to accommodate the context, but it's mostly the same in all styles. Singer Ex. 1 shows the basic pattern against a matching drum groove with a quarter-note hi-hat feel. This example shows how the pattern is typically written—but experiment with the variation shown in Singer Ex. 2, in which the dotted quarter-note is shortened to a quarter. This leaves space on beat *two* for the snare drum to sound by itself. If you are accurate in letting up on the quarter-note, the resulting rest creates a hole that lets the snare drum sit perfectly in the groove. Switch between Examples 1 and 2 and hear how the space affects the groove.

TRACK 13

Singer Ex. 1

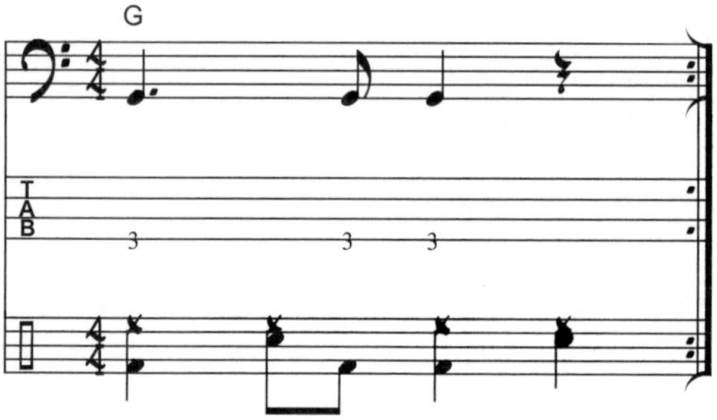

Singer Ex. 2

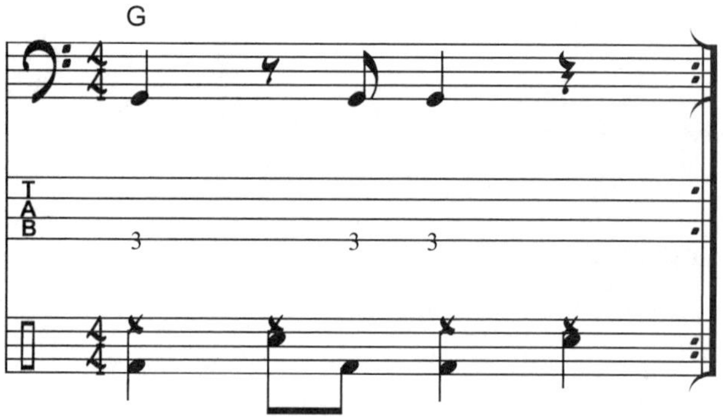

Changing the smallest rhythmic subdivisions can radically affect a groove. Singer Ex. 3 is the groove with an eighth-note hi-hat. Notice how the beats line up between the bass line and the drum part. Focus on nailing your eighth-note to the hi-hat pulse. Singer Ex. 4 shows the pattern with a 16th-note hi-hat. It's not uncommon for the bass to emphasize eighths while the drums play a 16th-note pulse. Notice how standing on the eighth-note grounds the pulse.

TRACK 13

Singer Ex. 3

Singer Ex. 4

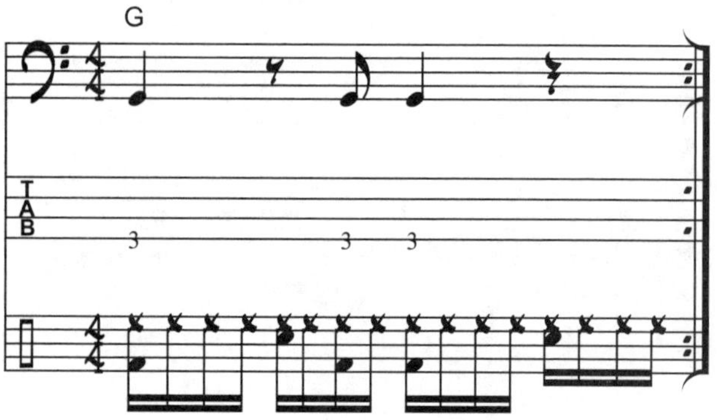

Ballads call for another interpretation of this rhythm. At a slow tempo you may choose to let the notes ring long, as leaving space for the snare drum may create too large a hole in the sonic spectrum. Singer Ex. 5 shows the line played with long notes at a ballad tempo.

Still another variation is heard in Brazilian music, most commonly the bossa nova (Singer Ex. 6). It's similar to a rock eighth-note feel, except that a clave (CLAH-vay) rhythm (played as a cross-stick) replaces the snare backbeat. Accent the ride cymbal on the clave beats, and listen to how the clave rhythm interacts with the bass part.

Singer Ex. 5

TRACK 13

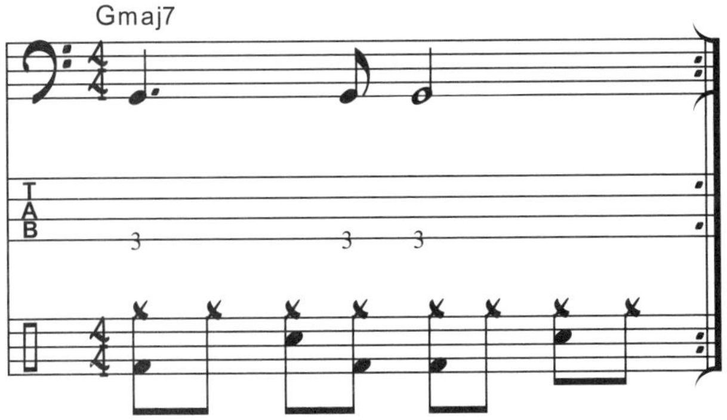

Singer Ex. 6

TRACK 13

Singer Drum Key

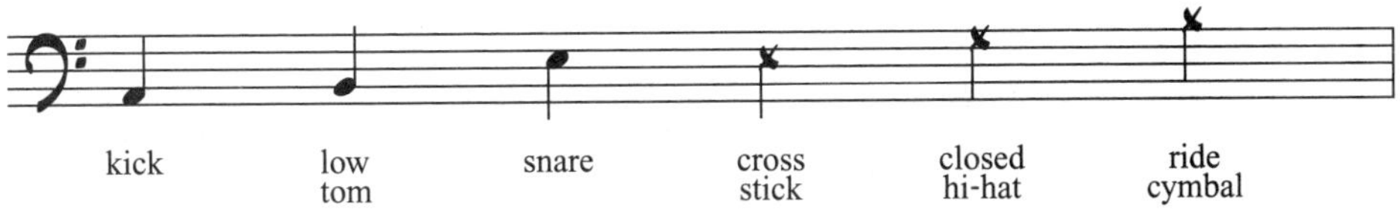

All of these examples have obvious similarities, and yet each is subtly different. Paying attention to these differences is what great bass playing is all about. Hey, what else are you going to do when you're stuck in a singer-songwriter groove for half an hour?

The Slow 12/8 Feel

Let's look at a cool groove that is deceptively challenging. The slow 12/8 is used in blues, gospel, R&B, pop, and many other styles. The tempos can run as low as quarter-note = 26 BPM! Fortunately the feel is usually subdivided, with the triplet played on the hi-hat or ride cymbal. This really helps you lock in.

By now you know that playing slowly and accurately can be even more challenging than playing fast. You are totally exposed, and any glitch in the hands or wavering of the beat is immediately noticeable. How do you pull it off? Relax, listen, and feel it. It helps if you can move your body; you literally have to dance through tempos like this. Swaying back and forth in tempo will help you get into it—but if you're playing a gospel gig, make sure you're swaying in the same direction as the choir! Some well-known examples of the slow 12/8 groove are Aretha Franklin's classic "(You Make Me Feel Like) a Natural Woman," Harold Melvin & the Blue Notes' "If You Don't Know Me by Now," the Eagles' "Take It to the Limit," and—the extreme end of the tempo spectrum—Ray Charles's live version of "Drown in My Own Tears."

The tricky thing about 12/8 is it can be written and interpreted two ways. When the time signature indicates 12/8, there are 12 eighth-notes per bar. This can be broken up in any configuration, but most often it conveys a triplet feel. What feels like a quarter-note is actually a dotted quarter, and the eighth-notes feel like triplets; 12/8 Ex. 1 shows how the groove is written in 12/8 time. It's common to write this in 4/4, with the ride cymbal or hi-hat notated as eighth-note triplets (12/8 Ex. 2). This is called "12/8 feel."

12/8 Ex. 1

12/8 Ex. 2

When programming this groove into your drum machine, set the pattern length for six beats and the quantization for eighth-notes. Most machines also allow you to set the value for the guide click, so set that to eighths, too. In 12/8 Ex. 3 you can see a simple bass line that works with this groove. The length of your notes is crucial at slow tempos, so hold the dotted half-notes for their full value. This approach is good for a full, broad sound—a "regal" sort of vibe. On bar 2's walk-down, pay attention to the articulations: The second note of the last group of eighth-notes should be shorter to give the last note some weight.

12/8 Ex. 3

TRACK 14

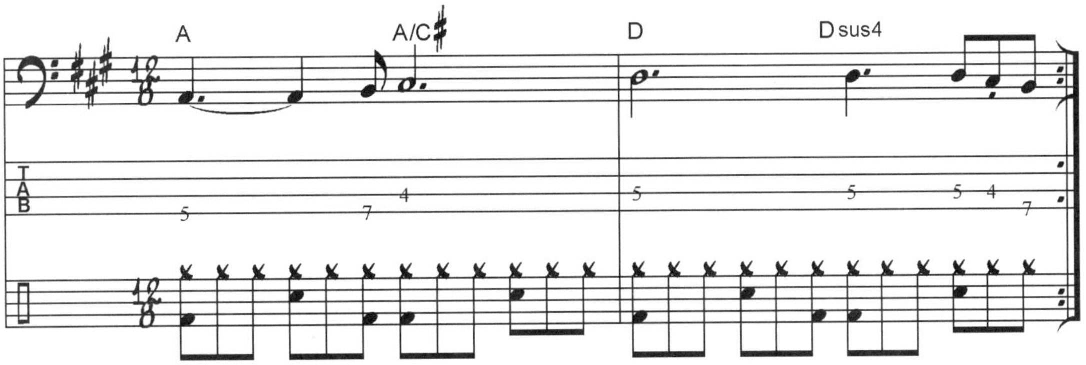

It's possible to get more active with this feel; drummers often emphasize a double-time undercurrent. This activity level is best illustrated in 12/8: Each eighth-note gets subdivided into a group of 16th-note triplets. Check 12/8 Ex. 4 for a slightly more active version of this groove. It looks busy, so remember that what feels like a quarter-note is actually worth three eighths. At a slow tempo the 16th-note triplets are easy to play. Bass solos are rare on such ballads, but we can still create a lot of drama by using rhythmic tricks like the short stop on bar 1's beat *two*. The space sets up the chromatic fill into beat *three*. This is a common fill, so don't be surprised if the keyboard player is right there with you on it. In bar 2 we create balance by starting out broadly on beat *one*, getting active on *two*, and broad again on *three*. Then the walk-down on beat *four* gets a lift by adding a rest and using a 16th-note triplet for the pickup. It's all very subtle, but, hey—if you're a bass player, subtle is your middle name, right?

12/8 Ex. 4

TRACK 14

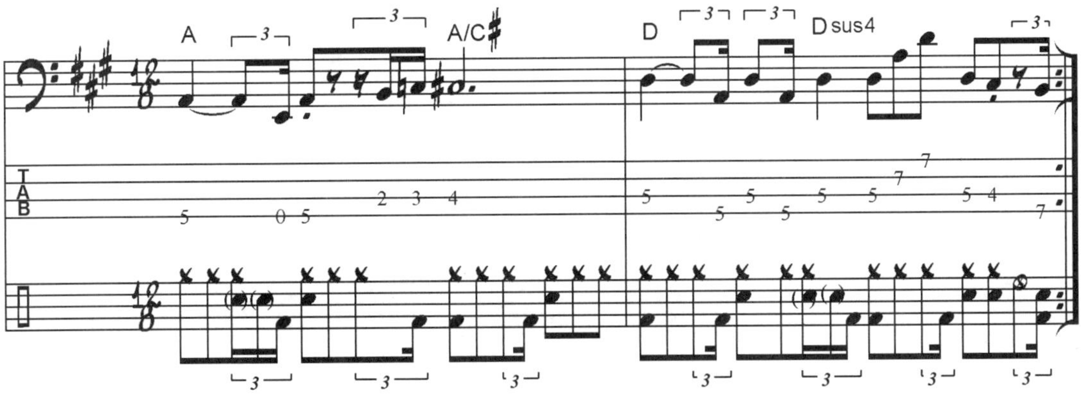

Experiment with this groove at tempos ranging from quarter-note = 30 BPM to 45 BPM. Above that, it becomes a whole different thing. Have fun with this one, and lay it down thick and smooth—like blackstrap molasses on a warm Memphis afternoon.

12/8 Drum Key

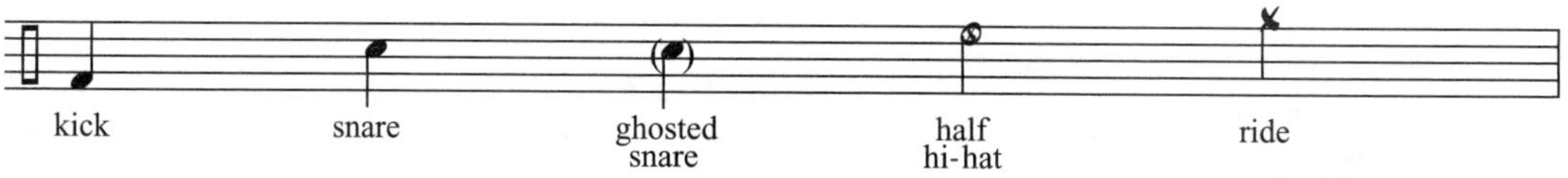

The Flat Tire Groove

There is a popular substyle of the blues idiom called "jump"—it's a place where swing jazz and early R&B meet. The overall feel is definitely swing-based, but the tunes are typically 12-bar blues, with perhaps the occasional I–VI–II–V progression thrown in. T-Bone Walker's famous "T-Bone Shuffle" and Louis Jordan's "Choo-Choo Ch'Boogie" are two classic examples of the genre. The underlying rhythm for this style is often called the "flat tire" groove because the drum part has the loping feel of a car driving with a flat. The bass plays a straight walking line and most often sticks with the classic 1–3–5–6–8–6–5–3 pattern typical of most swing music. The similarity to swing jazz makes it possible for many blues bands to function as "swing" groups and satisfy the jitterbug-crazed dance crowd that re-emerged in the '90s.

In the drum part the snare drum accents the second beat of an eighth-note triplet while the ride cymbal plays a swing pattern. Four-on-the-floor goes the kick drum, but don't play it too hard or it starts to sound like "house" music (Flat Ex. 1). The snare triplet on beat *four* of bar 2 should be dynamic: Hit the first snare around 50%, the second at 75%, and the last at 100%. The crescendo makes it feel authentic and pushes the groove forward. While it's written at the end of a two-bar phrase, you may want to program a four-bar pattern and just use the snare fill for the last measure.

Flat Ex. 1

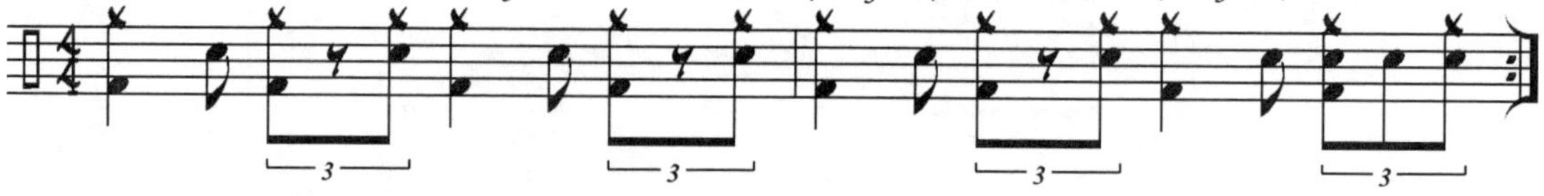

The bass line plays quarter-notes, but dig into the feel the snare accents create. Even though you're holding the quarter-note through it, the upbeat does influence your groove. There are a few possible lines that work with this style, but Flat Ex. 2 is a classic jump blues line with a II–V turnaround for the last four bars. It's in *A♭* because that's such a swingin' key—horn players love it, but guitar players will bemoan the loss of their beloved open *A* string. Too bad. You can make this groove come to life with the palm-muted/thumb-style technique that simulates the old "doghouse" upright sound of the jump-swing era.

TRACK 15

Flat Ex. 2

The Shuffle

The shuffle is one of the most familiar grooves. Its roots lie in African rhythms, and it was introduced into American popular music through the blues, which evolved into rhythm and blues and eventually rock 'n' roll. The shuffle has appeared in pop music in tunes as diverse as Smokey Robinson's "The Way You Do the Things You Do" and Alannah Myles's "Black Velvet." While both are a far cry from Muddy Waters, they owe their groove to the pioneering electric blues of postwar Chicago.

The shuffle is a triplet-based rhythm, with the first and third beats of an eighth-note triplet emphasized. If you divide a quarter-note in half, you get two even eighth-notes—but when you divide it into a triplet, you get three notes, each 33.333(. . .)% of a quarter-note's duration. That leftover bit of rhythmic "change" makes it an uneven split. This tiny remainder is where the magic of the shuffle exists, and it's why no two players sound exactly alike when playing it.

The shuffle rhythm gets interpreted either as staccato (short) or legato (long). At a slow tempo, practice playing the shuffle rhythm short and filling in the space by saying "chick" on the triplet's second beat—that helps keep the triplet feeling "round" (Shuffle Ex. 1). Give the offbeats a slight accent to push the groove forward.

Shuffle Ex. 1

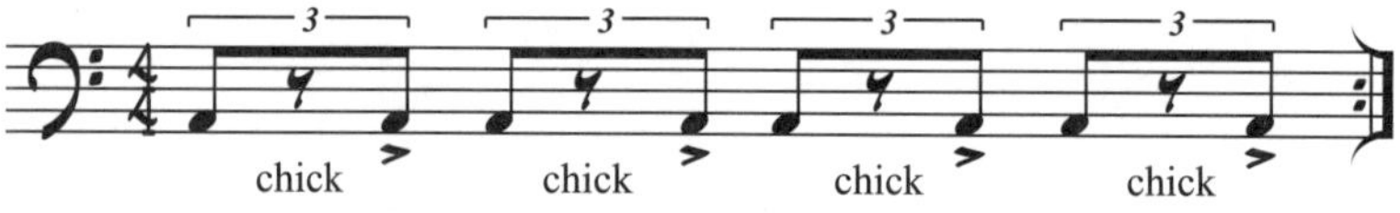

Let's look at a typical box-shape line played with a shuffle rhythm; this kind of line is commonly used to create a 12-bar blues by moving it through the I, IV, and V chords. Typical of a Chicago-style shuffle, the drum part for Shuffle Ex. 2 is also referred to as a shuffle "march." It helps to have two different snare drum sounds for this beat, one a looser, fat sound, and the other a rim-shot for the backbeats. The approximate dynamic levels for the snare are 75% for the hits on *one* and *three*, 50% for the offbeats, and 100% on the rim-shots on *two* and *four*. The example is written with a closed hi-hat sound, but you can substitute a ride cymbal. Tempo range is between 60 BPM and 140 BPM.

One way to determine whether to play long or short is to listen to the drum part: If the drummer is playing a tight shuffle on the hi-hat, it may be best to play the notes in the pattern short. This allows the space in the groove to create a contrast. If the drummer is playing the shuffle on the ride cymbal, long notes may work better by matching the cymbal's sustained sound. Let the first note ring for the triplet's first two beats, as in Shuffle Ex. 3. The change in note length has a big effect on the overall groove.

TRACK 16

Shuffle Ex. 2

Shuffle Ex. 3

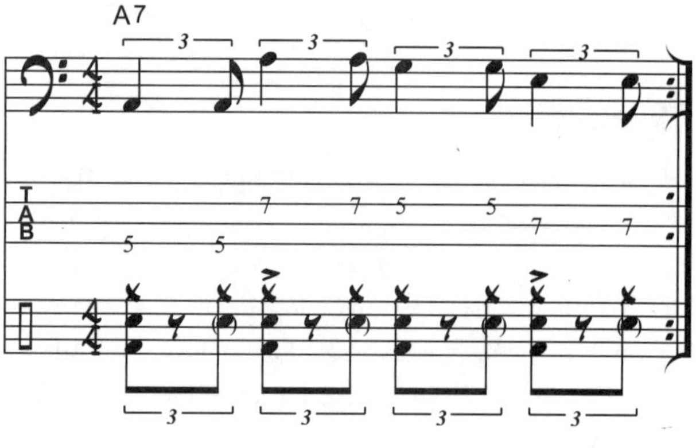

Another way to play a shuffle is to simply play quarter-notes. Sometimes the groove needs to breathe a bit—everyone hammering away at a shuffle can get oppressive. Shuffle Ex. 4a has the line played as quarter-notes; be sure you're hearing that "chick" internally—that keeps the groove rolling. The snare drum part is slightly altered to make this example a Texas shuffle. There is no snare hit right on *one* and *three*, just on the offbeats leading into and out of the backbeat. This puts more emphasis on the backbeat and makes the groove less march-like. Use these syllables to get the Texas shuffle groove into your head: "zing–ga–zack–ga–zing–ga–zack–ga." "Zack" is the snare drum on the backbeat. Shuffle Ex. 4b changes the ride cymbal to a swing pattern instead of the shuffle. This gives the groove a different character and works nicely at faster tempos.

Shuffle Ex. 4

TRACK 16

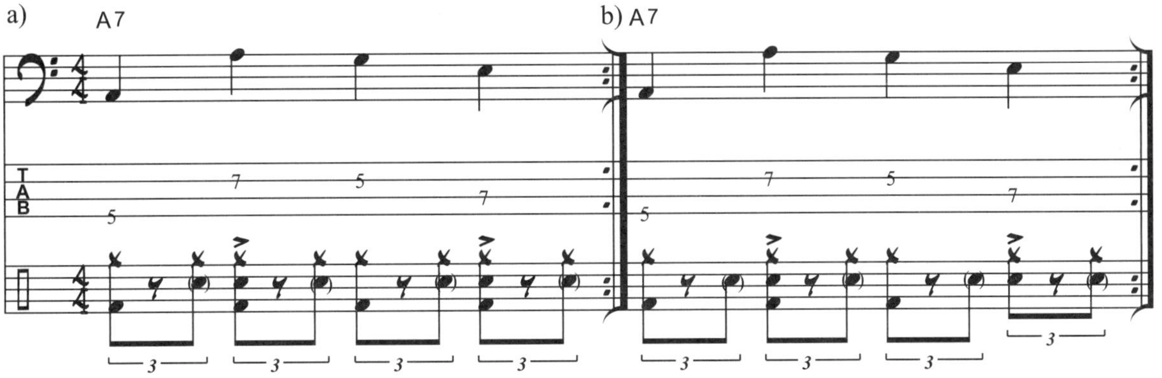

Another variation is the Kansas City shuffle. The hi-hat is either open or half open, depending on the sound you prefer, and it plays a swing rhythm instead of a shuffle. The offbeats on the snare are de-emphasized; you can also leave them out and use just the backbeat. For Shuffle Ex. 5, the bass line is the classic 1–3–5–6–8–6–5–3 pattern. It gives the blues the jazz flavor that helped artists like Big Joe Turner and Jay McShann bridge the gap between swing and rock 'n' roll.

Shuffle Ex. 5

TRACK 16

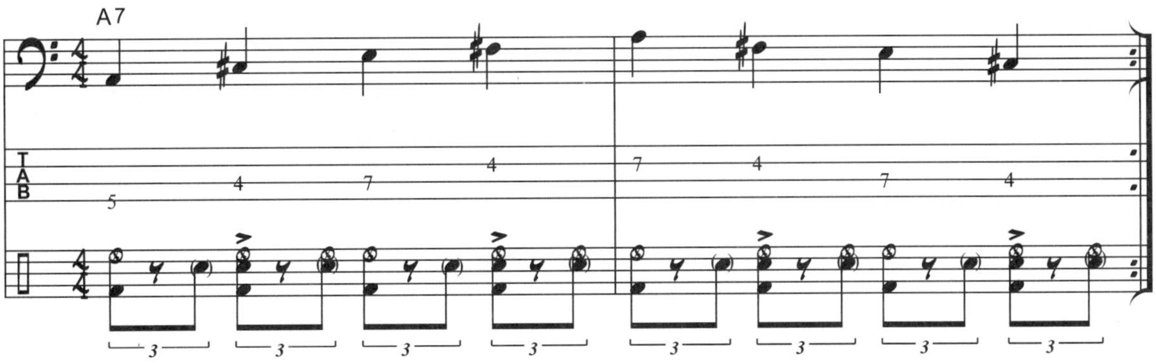

Practice the shuffle at a variety of tempos, and listen to a range of blues artists to pick up on the regional variations. While the drums have more to do with the differences in these grooves, to fully capture the flavor the bass must adapt itself in subtle ways, too.

The Anticipated Backbeat

In 90% of Western popular music, we hear the snare drum played on the backbeats (beats *two* and *four*)—but not in this groove, where the backbeat is anticipated by a 16th-note. This creates a hip, lopsided effect. The snare can anticipate *two* or *four*, or both. To lock in, you need to become totally comfortable with the dotted-eighth/16th rhythm. AB Ex. 1 demonstrates the rhythm with the syllables "oo–ka–chu–bop"; for the left-brain crowd, these syllables correspond to the rhythmic breakdown of "one–e–and–a," which is how we're usually taught to count four 16th-notes. Turn on your metronome or drum machine and practice speaking "oo-ka-chu-bop" in tempo. Notice how the last syllable naturally gets a little accent—in this groove, that will become our new backbeat.

AB Ex. 2 breaks this down to syllables again. Say "oo–ka–chu–ba–ding" in tempo to get the feel of it. The "ba" of beat *one* needs to line up perfectly, and it also must release precisely into the "ding" on beat *two*. It may seem silly to use these syllables, but they're more intuitive than "one–e–and–a, two–e–and–a." They are also the basis of drum language, which you need to learn if you want to communicate with our percussively inclined brothers and sisters. The good news is drum language can be made up as you go along—all you need to do is find a way to sing a rhythm accurately, and you've got it. Take any drum groove and find a way to distill the parts into a speech pattern. You may sound like a lunatic while doing it, but soon you'll see why all drummers understand it!

AB Ex. 1

AB Ex. 2

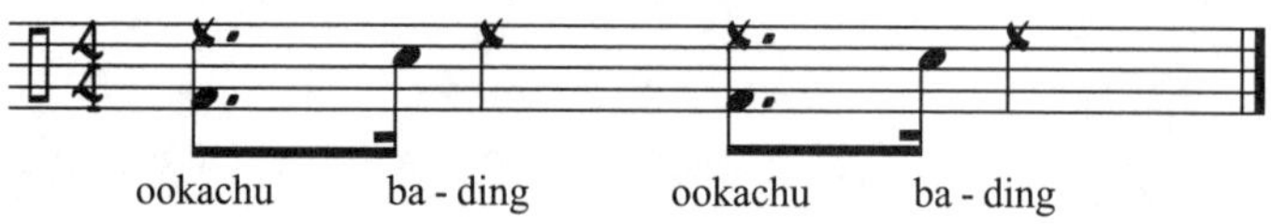

AB Ex. 3 is a typical bass/drum groove using the anticipated backbeat. Notice how the bass line uses an octave on the "bop" of beat *one* to emphasize the hit. This works well if you're slapping—but slapping is optional; you can play this fingerstyle too. The hi-hat plays quarter-notes in this example. Notice how the beats line up in the drum part. See how the anticipated snare lands right before the hi-hat on *two*? Feeling the space in between these two beats is critical to nailing this groove.

AB Ex. 4 puts the anticipation on the "bop" of beat *three*. Because the first backbeat is in its typical place on *two*, it sets up the expectation that the second backbeat will be typical, as well. When the second backbeat anticipates, it creates a cool, jerky feel. When you play this example, feel how the rhythm is interpreted in the body—or as Otis Redding so aptly put it, put your hand on your hip and let your backbone slip!

AB Ex. 3

TRACK 17

AB Ex. 4

TRACK 17

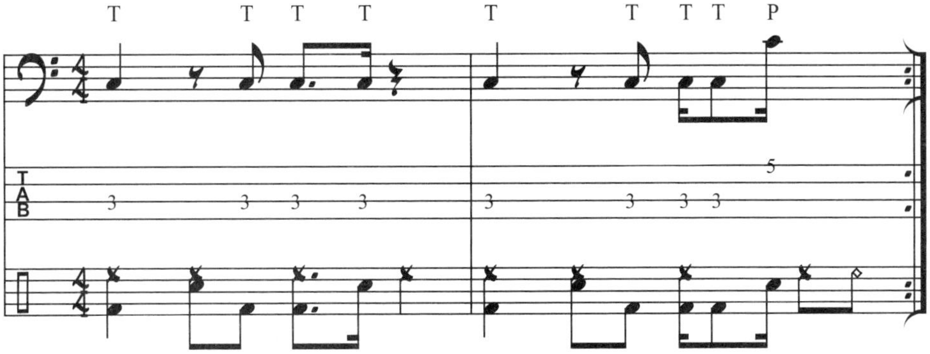

AB Ex. 5 anticipates both backbeats. While this may be a bit much for a whole tune, you do hear it sometimes. With 16th-notes on the hi-hat and toms on the backbeats, it becomes a popular Afro-Caribbean groove (AB Ex. 6).

AB Ex. 5

TRACK 17

TRACK 17

AB Ex. 6

Take all of these drum patterns and experiment with eighths and 16ths on the hi-hat. Try your own rhythms on the kick drum, add snare hits—you learn more about a groove by pushing it to its limits. Of course, when it's time to play, you want to make sure you're not sacrificing the feel for the sake of complexity. Have fun with this one!

The James Brown Groove

Few artists have had as huge an impact on modern popular music as James Brown—the Man with the Master Plan, the Big Bad Boss with the Real Hot Sauce, Butane James & His Famous Flames—or simply, the Godfather of Soul. While his early hits like "It's a Man's Man's Man's World," "I'll Go Crazy," and "Please Please Please" are brilliant examples of the early R&B 12/8 feel, it wasn't until 1967's "Cold Sweat" that JB drummer Clyde Stubblefield recorded what would ultimately become known as the "James Brown groove." This feel's key element is delaying the second backbeat of bar 1 to the "and" of beat *four*. This delay creates suspense and drama; it's the kind of moment that calls for a nasty horn punch—or, if you can muster up the funk, a visceral "*unnh!*" Programming this groove into your drum machine will require touch sensitivity, as ghost-notes on the snare drum are crucial to the feel. JB Ex. 1 is the basic drum groove; it's similar to the feel on "Cold Sweat," "Mother Popcorn," and other classic JB hits.

JB Ex. 1

JB Ex. 2 is a generic version of the bass part that fits this groove. James Brown's music features specific parts that create the tune's signature. While similar, "Cold Sweat" and "Mother Popcorn" have different bass lines. If you're called upon to play a JB-style groove, JB Ex. 2 will fulfill all the requirements. In this two-bar pattern, the first bar uses the delayed snare hit on the "and" of *four*, one of the elements that bring the groove together. Make sure you feel the missing hit on *four*; this will help you "spring" into the upbeat with assurance. Bar 2 typically features a syncopated "walk-up" pattern from the 3rd of the chord.

JB Ex. 3 is the same basic line but with the notes played short. Feel the difference the space creates in the groove. This time the bar 2 walk-up has a few added 16th-notes to enhance the staccato feel.

JB Ex. 2

TRACK 18

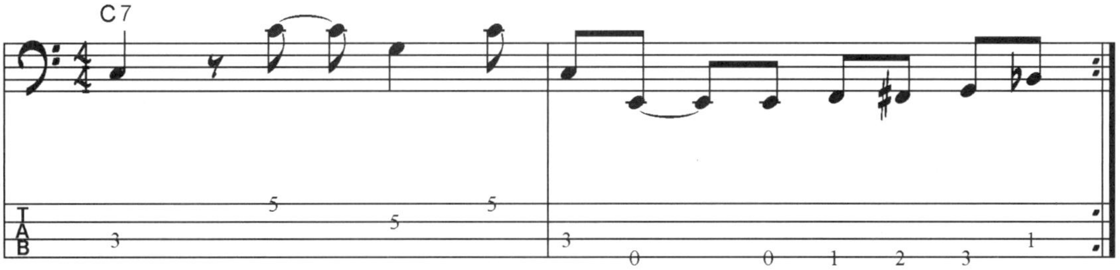

JB Ex. 3

TRACK 18

JB Ex. 4, a more active variation, uses ghost-notes to pull the bass line together with the snare drum. This four-bar version shows two variations in the phrase's second half. Bar 2 has a neat stuttering walk-up. Bar 4 is a cool Chuck Rainey–inspired fill that would be great to throw in at the end of an eight-bar phrase. Don't use it too much—maybe twice in a whole tune.

JB Ex. 4

TRACK 18

James Brown's music got even funkier as time progressed, but this early groove provided the genetic code for funk. It still packs the dance floor, sending the lower lumbar region into spasmodic contortions. It has been sampled to death by rappers and hip-hoppers and sped up to maniacal tempos by the drum-n-bass crowd. For more information and grooves, check out the definitive source on James Brown's music: *The Funkmasters: The Great James Brown Rhythm Sections 1960–1973* by Allan "Dr. Licks" Slutsky and Chuck Silverman [Warner Bros.].

The Bo Diddley Beat

This groove segment is sponsored by Bo Diddley, the man who made it cool to shake maracas while wearing plaid. The groove is rooted in Afro-Caribbean culture as the 3:2 clave pattern—see Bo Ex. 1. The rhythm found its way into American popular music through New Orleans, where African and Caribbean cultures influenced jazz, R&B, and rock 'n' roll. The Bo Diddley groove can be found in music by artists such as the Neville Brothers ("Iko Iko"), Bow Wow Wow ("I Want Candy," originally recorded in 1965 by the Strangeloves), and, of course, Diddley himself ("Hey! Bo Diddley").

Bo Ex. 1

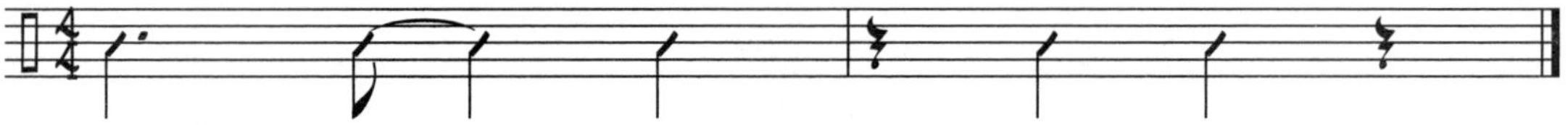

Let's look at a few applications for this groove and its variations. The tempos range from 130 BPM on the slow end to 240 BPM. Bo Ex. 2 shows the basic groove with a simplified New Orleans second-line drum pattern. When programming your drum machine, pay careful attention to the accents in the snare drum part; they're critical to this groove's success. Keep the velocity (volume) of the ghosted, unaccented snare hits low; they serve more as filler than actual beats. Use two snare drum sounds if you can; play the ghost-notes on the loose snare and the accents on a rim-shot or harder sound. If you want to experiment, try assigning the eighth-notes a swing factor between 58% and 64%—this gives the groove a completely different feel.

TRACK 19

Bo Ex. 2

As always, the bass part's note length is crucial. Bo Ex. 2 is written "long," with the note duration taking up the space. This works well for keeping the feel broad and open. To tighten up the groove for a funkier feel, play it short, as in Bo Ex. 3.

Bo Ex. 3

TRACK 19

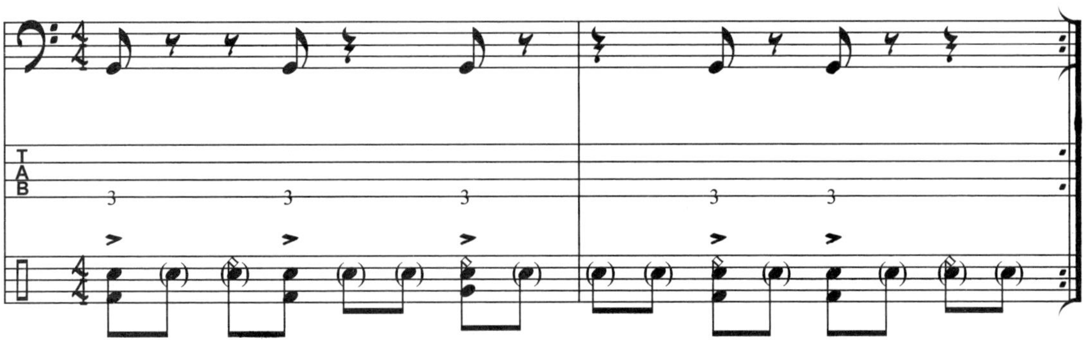

Bo Ex. 4 shows a version embellished with ghost-notes and fills at the end of bars 2 and 4. This groove is a great springboard for funk. Check out some of the New Orleans funk masters like Dr. John, the Neville Brothers, the Meters, and the Wild Tchoupitoulas to hear the groove being funkified to death.

Bo Ex. 4

TRACK 19

Bo Ex. 5 is a more intricate swinging-funk version. The drum part is written in eighth-notes, but to achieve the swing feel, program a 68% swing factor. I've written the bass part in straight eighths, but you should play it with swing—you'll know what to do when you hear the drums. Notice how the groove gets filled out with left-hand slapped ghost-notes. This feel is tailor-made for evil slapping.

TRACK 19

Bo Ex. 5

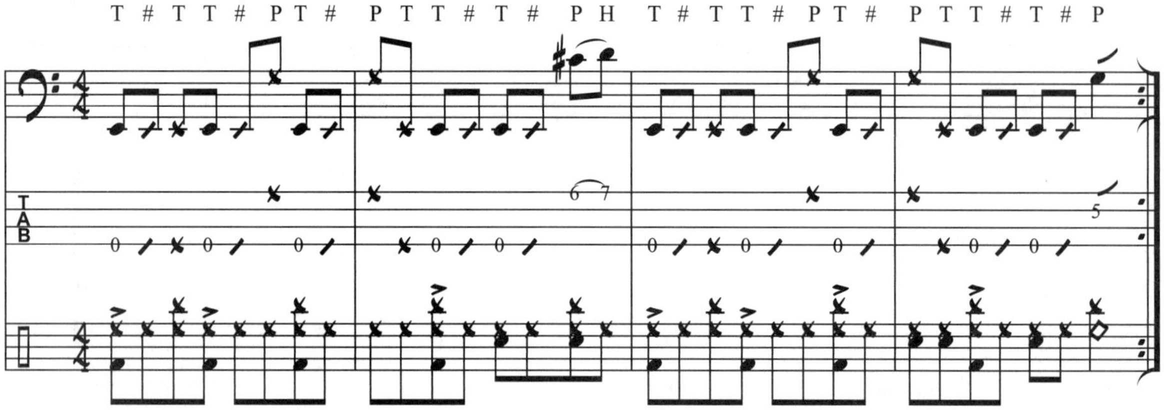

Bo Diddley Drum Key

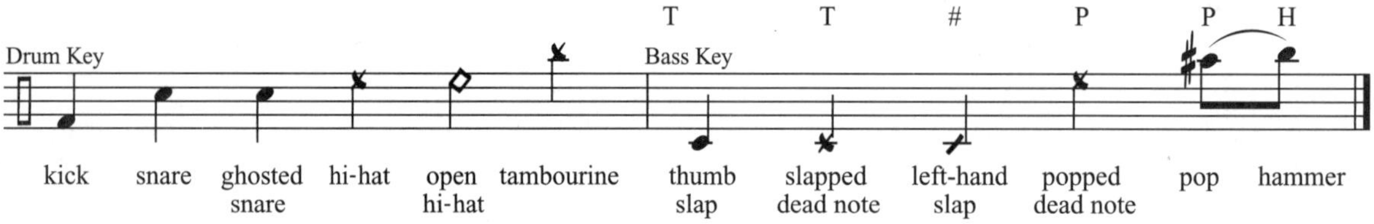

Have fun with the Bo Diddley groove—it's a classic that shows up every few years in a hit song. It even fueled teeny-bopper Aaron Carter's recent rise to the top of pop with his version of "I Want Candy." Careful, Aaron—that stuff'll rot yer teeth!

Rockin' Rhumba

This groove has similarities to the Bo Diddley feel. It has the same rhythm as the Diddley groove's first measure, with the bass line ascending a major-triad arpeggio. You've heard this one a million times in rock 'n' roll, rockabilly, Cajun, Latin, country, reggae, and other styles. Like the Diddley groove, its roots are in the groove-fertile Caribbean; it was introduced in this country by Afro-Caribbean transplants who made New Orleans their home. These syncopated ethnic strains crossbred with European harmonies, forming the mother lode of ideas that became jazz, R&B, and rock 'n' roll.

Rhumba Ex. 1 is the simple bass line. Think of Elvis's version of the Big Mama Thornton classic "Hound Dog" or the Grateful Dead's cover of Bobby Bland's "Turn on Your Love Light." It can be played both long (Rhumba Ex. 1) or short (Rhumba Ex. 2).

Rhumba Ex. 1

TRACK 20

Rhumba Ex. 2

TRACK 20

Since the bass part doesn't change in this groove, let's try a few drum feels with it. Rhumba Ex. 3 is a straight beat: The kick drum catches the rhythm with the bass line. It can work with many different styles. For Rhumba Ex. 4, try this experiment: Play it as written with straight eighth-notes, and then set your drum machine's swing factor to around 67% for the eighth-note—it's amazing how the whole groove changes.

Rhumba Ex. 3

Rhumba Ex. 4

TRACK 20

Rhumba Ex. 5a is a swinging R&B feel; set the drum machine's quantization to eighth-note triplets to program this groove. You can play it from 90 BPM to 170 BPM. Changing the ride-cymbal pattern to a side-stick will give the groove a rockabilly flavor (5b). If your machine has a flam button, program the side-stick with it—it will sound like the real deal. Change the ride pattern to a closed hi-hat for a tighter sound (5c).

TRACK 20

Rhumba Ex. 5

Rhumba Ex. 6 is a New Orleans "second line" parade beat. Touch sensitivity is important for the snare-drum pattern—the accents make it work. For best results, use the two-snare drum approach. Set the ghosted filler snare on a loose, fat sound at approximately 55% volume, and the accent beats on a rim-shot at 100%. You can also experiment with different accents on the ghosted snare part. Switch the quantization to 16th-note triplets to program the snare triplet at the end of bar 2. Play it in slowly and try to make each note of the figure progressively louder.

TRACK 20

Rhumba Ex. 6

Rhumba Ex. 7 is a Latin feel that can be used on casual gigs. (When the old guy in the kelly-green pants asks for a rhumba, this is what he'll get!) Play the 16th-note triplet softly on the snare; if you can control the dynamics, make the triplet crescendo from piano to forte. Switch the quantization to straight 16ths for the rest of the pattern. It's a cheesy groove, but hey—cheesy is cool! (Try playing rhumba versions of your favorite Ramones tunes.)

Rhumba Ex. 7

TRACK 20

Rhumba Ex. 8 is a classic '50s rock 'n' roll groove; picture all the kids at the malt shop havin' a ball to this one. Rhumba Ex. 9 is a dancehall-style reggae groove. Many contemporary drum machines have a kit that sounds like the old Roland TR–808; use that and lock into this one for 30 minutes—you'll be jammin'.

Rhumba Ex. 8

TRACK 20

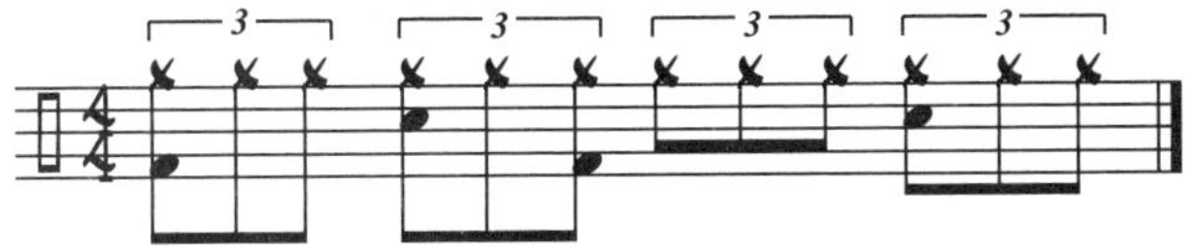

Rhumba Ex. 9

TRACK 20

Rhumba Drum Key

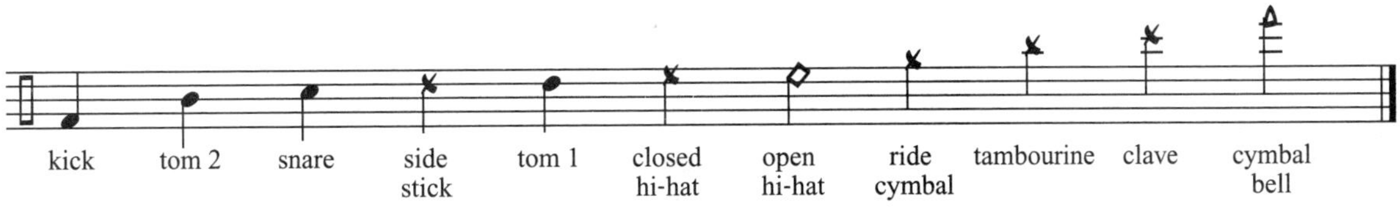

As you can see, this humble little bass line covers a lot of ground. That's one of the great things about bass playing—it's universal. Bassists in all styles do the same job: We mind the form, play the root, and make it groove. We may even be playing the same line from style to style, although the other instrumental parts may be totally different. This is what gives us so much flexibility in the music world. All one, on the *one!*

The Fats Domino 12/8 Groove

Once again we return to New Orleans, the cradle of rock 'n' roll (and jazz), to find a groove that fueled many of the early rock hits and that's continually recycled by blues and R&B groups. The 12/8 Fats Domino groove is found on some of his classic hits like "Blueberry Hill," "Ain't That a Shame," and "Blue Monday," as well as tracks by many other New Orleans artists such as Smiley Lewis and Irma Thomas. It became more mainstream behind songs like "The Great Pretender" by the Platters and "Earth Angel" by the Penguins. A great modern-day representation of this feel is "Get Over Me" by Sugar Ray & the Bluetones.

One of the main elements of this groove is the piano slamming out straight triplets with the right hand, matching the ride or hi-hat cymbal, with the left hand often doubling the bass line. The guitar most often hits the chords on *two* or *four* backbeats. The bass line has a few variations but will get its melodic shape from the triad. This groove is typically notated as "12/8 feel": Using 4/4 as the time signature, each quarter-note is subdivided into eighth-note triplets, giving you the same amount of beats per bar as 12/8. The advantage to this notation is you can clearly see the downbeats of beats *one*, *two*, *three*, and *four* represented in the bar.

Fats Ex. 1 is a simple version of the bass line going straight up and down the triad. Make sure to leave the space on *two* for the snare drum. The drum part is written with the ride cymbal playing the triplets, but you can substitute it with the closed hi-hat for a tighter feel. You might want to use a hi-hat on the song's verse and then switch to the ride cymbal to "open up" the chorus.

TRACK 21

Fats Ex. 1

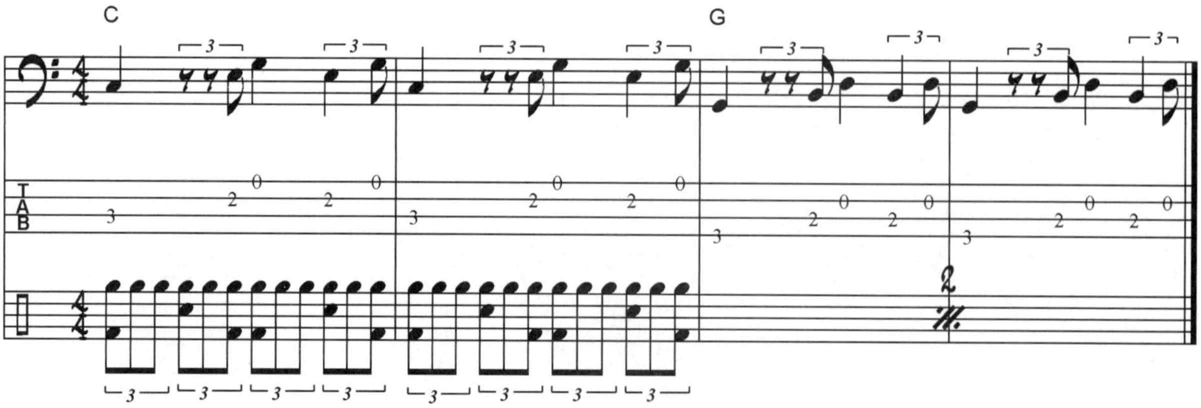

Fats Ex. 2 adds the octave on the backbeat, giving the feel a little "goose." Sometimes the guitar will double this line to fill out the sound. Fats Ex. 3 is a little busier, doubling up the 5th of the chord. Bar 3 holds yet another variation, a scale line from the 3rd to the 5th over a triplet rhythm that can be used to fill out the groove even more.

Fats Ex. 2

TRACK 21

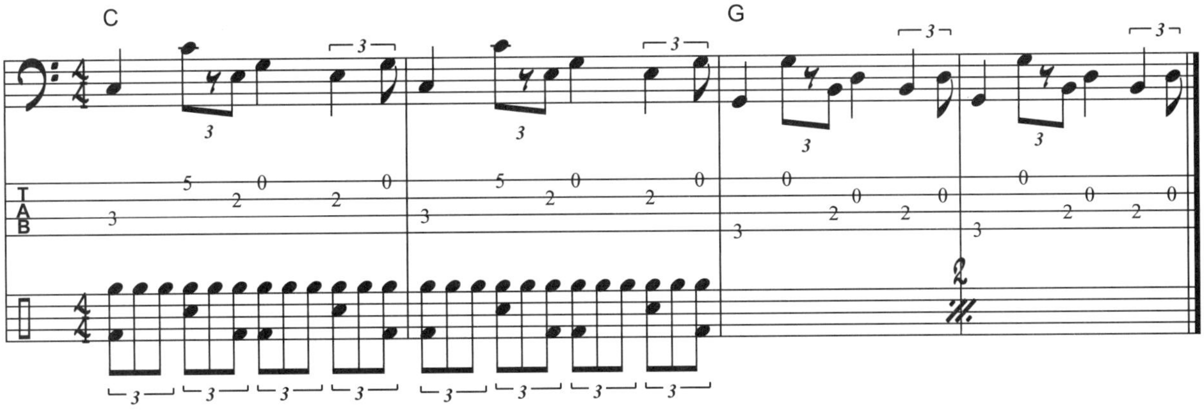

Fats Ex. 3

TRACK 21

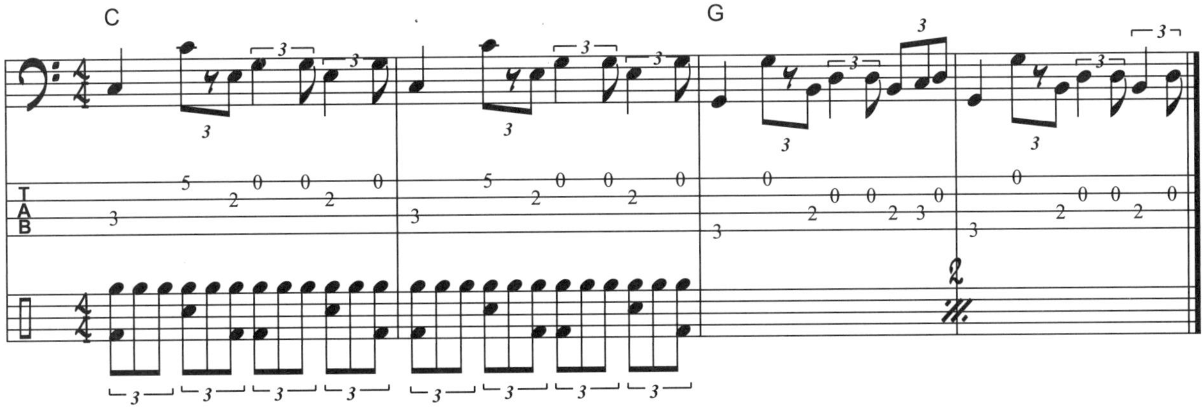

These variations are somewhat interchangeable, but you should commit to one or the other for a section or a whole chorus. Random switching of bass patterns will make a groove like this sound unsettled.

Slow Blues

Let's get down and dirty with some slow blues. While shuffles and "Tramp" grooves are the mainstay of all blues bands' repertoire, each night the moment inevitably comes when it's time to testify, time to take it way down, bring the lights on down behind me, boys . . . time for a slow blues. While most everyone is familiar with the 12-bar blues form, playing it at tempos as slow as 30 BPM presents a unique challenge. You are totally exposed to the elements with no place to hide. Every note you play is right up front; you can't take anything back. Your note choices have to be perfect, your time must be rock solid, note length is critical, and you must follow the dynamic flow of the performance. A lead singer will milk a slow blues for every last drop of "show-bidness" excitement—you'll have to build it up at the slightest hint of emotion and break it down at the drop of a hat. You may have to catch kicks signaled by a hand, foot, head, or guitar neck without missing a beat. For all these reasons (and more), the slow blues is the ultimate test of a bass player's ability to groove.

As in a shuffle, the slow blues is eighth-note-triplet based, but the ride cymbal or hi-hat will play a solid 12/8 feel, breaking up each quarter-note evenly. The snare is on the backbeat, and the kick plays the big downbeats of *one* and *three* with an eighth-note-triplet pickup. The cymbal may sometimes break up the triplet as in the slow gospel 12/8 feel, but for this example, program this basic feel (Slow Ex. 1) into your drum machine. It will help you to have a steady and predictable cushion to work out this groove.

Slow Ex. 1

Slow Ex. 2 is a chorus of blues in G. The tempo can range from quarter-note equals 30 BPM to as high as 60 BPM. Faster than 60 BPM it becomes more like a Fats Domino groove, and you would play a completely different line. The drums push this groove along. Much of the time the bass is holding long tones; you'll have to feel the triplet pulse from the cymbal. When you do get rhythmic, it needs to be dead-on accurate and have the swinging quality the triplet demands. Don't try to be cute and play straight eighths or 16ths—that's *not* clever, it's distracting. Remember that everything you play is under the microscope; this is not the time to introduce any foreign microorganisms.

Bars 1 and 2 are straightforward. Start at mezzo-piano (which literally means "half-soft"), and play everything nice and long. In bar 3 you go up to the V7 chord on beat *three*, a good way to break up the space of what is usually two bars of the I7. This creates a mini-cadence and gives the progression some momentum. In bar 4 lay down the low G with authority, follow the rise in volume with the octave G, and play it like it's going to do something big—the triplet on *four* should build up to the forte marking on beat *one* of bar 5. In bar 5, cut the quarter-note off right on the backbeat. The snare will hit hard, and the whole band will suddenly drop back to *piano*; it's very dramatic—and the oldest trick in the book. Bar 6 smoothes out the feel with some fat quarter-notes; play the triplet notes nice and long, too. In bar 8 the line gets into the shuffle rhythm for the buildup. Make sure you leave the rest blank; the space is necessary to give the line contrast. On beat *four* play the triplet long and smooth, and cruise into that V7 chord in bar 9 at mezzo-forte—you ain't home yet! The triplet on beat *four* is accented and sets up the IV7 chord nicely. Play the quarter-notes in bar 10 broadly and get ready for the big buildup for the turnaround in bars 11 and 12. The crescendo should peak on beat *three* of bar 12, and once again the snare on beat *four* will bring it down to mezzo-forte for the pickups to the top of the form. Drop it back to mezzo-piano for the repeat.

Wheeew! That's a lot of action in a small space. In 12 bars you've given the audience a ride on the blues emotional rollercoaster, up . . . down . . . up . . . down . . . enough already! When you lay it down behind a great singer, this dynamic approach to the blues is a sure crowd pleaser. The most common intro for a slow blues is to start from the V7 chord in bar 9 with a guitar solo, and then the singer comes in at the top of the form. It goes something like this: "Slow blues in G, from the V: one . . . two . . . three . . . bom–bom–bom . . ."

TRACK 22

Slow Ex. 2

Pumpin' Eighths

One of the most common activities in rock and R&B bass playing is pumping out eighth-notes. Thousands of mega-hits have had this simple yet effective approach to the bottom line—it's a must-know style. Though it's basic, this approach requires solid time and technical consistency to make it happen. You can also vary the eighth-notes in several ways to create dramatically different feels. Let's start with the drums. Pumpin' Ex. 1 shows you the basic beat: kick on *one* and *three*, snare on *two* and *four*, and the hi-hat playing eighth-notes. Play the hi-hat downbeats separately on the first pass at 100%, then do the upbeats (the "ands") hitting the pads at around 85% of their volume sensitivity. This makes the part sound less mechanical. You can also drastically change the groove by using different hi-hat sounds. First program the beat with a nice tight closed hi-hat (1a). Then try switching to a half-closed hi-hat—it's a completely different vibe, just a little heavier (1b). Try the open hi-hat next (1c); if you can adjust the volume of the hi-hat separately, bring it down a little so it doesn't overpower everything. These variations all have noticeable effects on the groove.

By working with dynamics, you can change things even more. Further softening the upbeats gives you a cool R&B flavor (Pumpin' Ex. 2). Start by programming in the downbeats at full volume, then play the upbeats on the second pass through the pattern at approximately 65% volume. It lets the pattern breath a bit, as opposed to the steady pulse of Ex. 1.

TRACK 23

Pumpin' Ex. 1

TRACK 23

Pumpin' Ex. 2

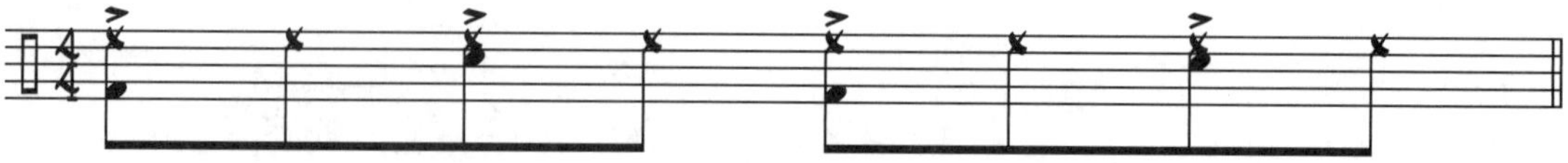

Pumpin' Ex. 3 shows a simple two-chord progression with the bass slamming out the eighths and sticking to the root. The tempo can range from 60 to 145 BPM. When playing this example fingerstyle, alternate between your index and middle fingers and strive for consistent volume and tone. If you're playing it pickstyle, try the line with all downstrokes as well as with alternate picking. It's interesting to see how different each variation can sound: using a pick or fingers; closed, half-open, or open hi-hat; with different degrees of accent on the downbeats; and, of course, with widely different tempos. That's probably why this approach gets used so often; it easily adapts itself to different vibes without major changes to the parts.

Pumpin' Ex. 3

TRACK 23

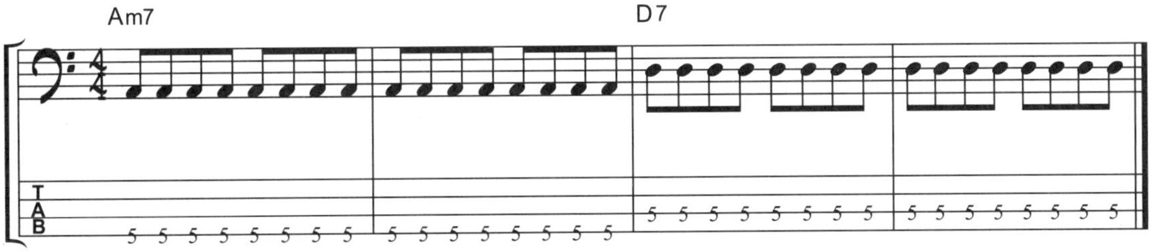

In Pumpin' Ex. 4 the notes are played staccato, or short. You can achieve this fingerstyle by muting the string between strokes with the next finger. Play a note with your index finger, then place your middle finger on the string a little early in preparation for the next note. This creates a space between notes and gives the line a distinctly different feel. Playing pickstyle, you can do this by resting the palm of your right hand on the strings just in front of the bridge. Muting with different degrees of pressure creates very different sounds. This technique is a mainstay of rock bass playing.

Pumpin' Ex. 4

TRACK 23

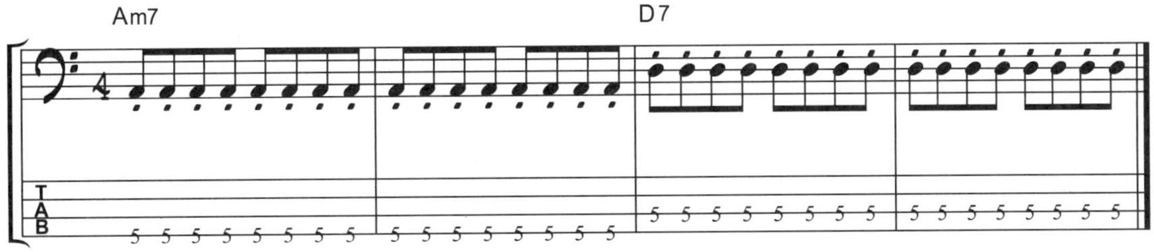

Using accents in the bass line also makes for interesting variations. Pumpin' Ex. 5 places the accents on beat *two* and the "ands" of beats *three* and *four*. This gives the line a strong push into the next measure. In the drum part, experiment with doubling the upbeat accents on different drums. Try the snare, toms, kick, even a crash cymbal—they each have their own character.

There are many ways to vary this line with melodic devices. Pumpin' Ex. 6 adds a melodic anticipation that matches the upbeat accents.

TRACK 23

Pumpin' Ex. 5

TRACK 23

Pumpin' Ex. 6

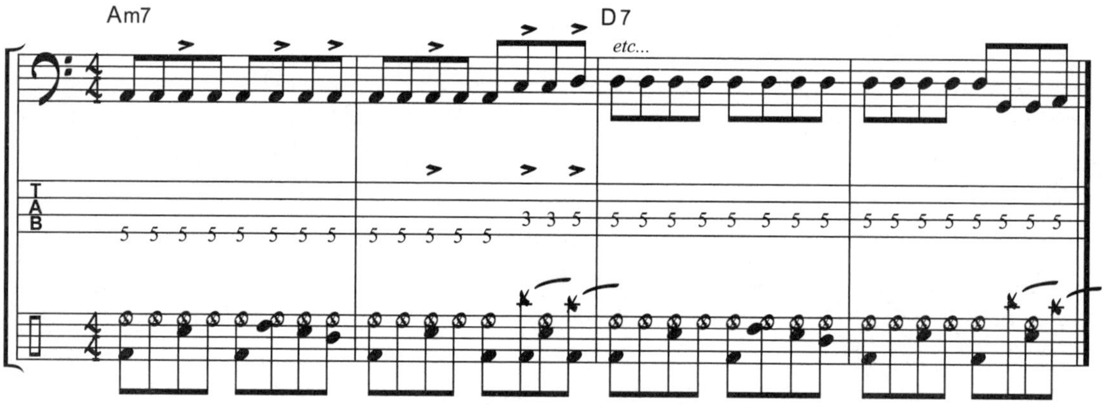

Pumpin' Ex. 7 puts staccato notes and accents together to create a cool R&B feel that sounds a bit like an Al Green groove. Play the downbeats short and quieter than the upbeats—this has a "backward" feel that really kicks the groove forward. For the true Al Green experience, put the downbeat's heavy hi-hat rhythm on a floor tom instead. Look for a tom sound that has a nice attack, medium decay, and medium pitch so it won't get too muddy. Once you have it dialed in, it's "Love and Happiness" for days.

Experiment with different accents, lines, and drum parts; you'll find that pumping eighth-notes can be a lot more interesting than you may have thought.

Pumpin' Ex. 7

TRACK 23

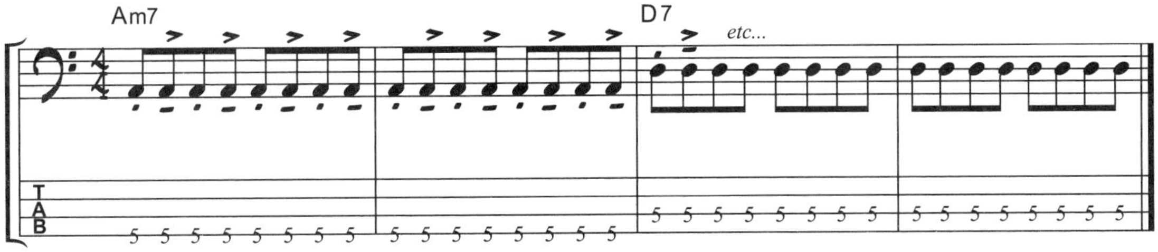

Pumpin' Drum Key

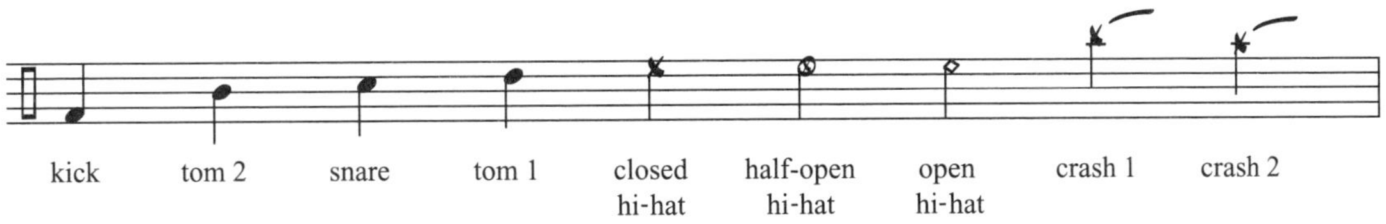

The Twist

The twist was an early '60s dance craze that left an indelible stamp on rock 'n' roll. Although "The Twist" was written and recorded by Hank Ballard & the Midnighters in 1958, Chubby Checker's 1960 recording is more widely known. The rhythmic elements of the Twist can be found in earlier New Orleans R&B, fueling '50s hits like Little Richard's "Lucille" and Huey "Piano" Smith's "Don't You Just Know It." The Twist beat made its way to the West Coast, launching the careers of many surf-rock bands with hits such as the Surfaris' 1963 classic, "Wipeout."

The twist groove is still widely used in many genres, and although there is no definitive twist bass line, there are a few common approaches you should know. Twist Ex. 1 is the classic twist drumbeat; the eighth-notes can be played on the hi-hat (1a) or ride cymbal (1b). Experiment with the differences between closed, half-open, and open hi-hats.

Twist Ex. 2 shows the New Orleans twist, a cool variation that puts the eighth-notes on the snare drum. Programming this beat requires good control over pad sensitivity. If your drum machine allows you to create your own drum kits, set up one with two snare drums to simulate the different tones live drummers get out of the snare. Make one snare a harder, rim-shot-type sound for the accented beats and the other looser and slightly lower-pitched to fill out the eighth-notes. If you can't set up a two-snare kit, program all the eighth-notes in at 60% pad sensitivity on the first pass. On beat *two* the snare should be roughly 85%, and on the upbeat of *two* and downbeat of *four* at 100% volume. These dynamics also apply if you program the hits on a separate snare sound. Experiment with adding swing to either drum beat; 54% on the eighth-notes will loosen it up nicely, while 58% will make it a border-line shuffle feel. The pedal hi-hat on the quarter-note keeps the feel moving.

TRACK 24

Twist Ex. 1

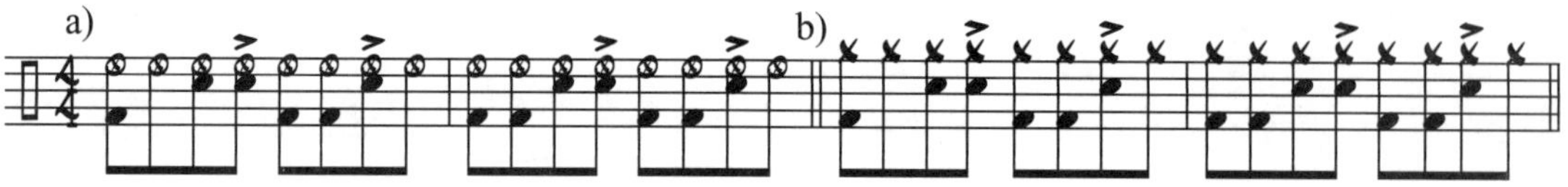

TRACK 24

Twist Ex. 2

Twist Ex. 3 is a pumping eighth-note line that uses a classic R&B melodic shape—the root down to the 6, down to the 5, and back up. It works great with a Chubby Checker vibe.

Twist Ex. 4 is a bit more surfy, using the ♭7 and moving down to the 5 and back up with a chromatic line. The quarter-note on *one* gives the groove a chance to breath, but it's fine to play two eighth-notes instead.

TRACK 24

Twist Ex. 3

TRACK 24

Twist Ex. 4

With a Little Richard vibe similar to "Lucille," Twist Ex. 5 works great with the New Orleans twist beat. It's tricky for the left (fretting) hand. You need to start on your 2nd finger to play up the major triad, but that leaves you going back and forth between the octave and ♭7 with the 2nd and 4th fingers. Then you have to skip back down very quickly from the ♭7 to the root with the 2nd finger. It's a challenge to make those moves smoothly; with the root on the downbeat of bar 2 you don't want it to sound awkward. Hint: Play the last ♭7 in the middle of your 2nd finger, near the first knuckle. That gives you a head start to roll across the *D* string to catch the root.

Twist Ex. 5

TRACK 24

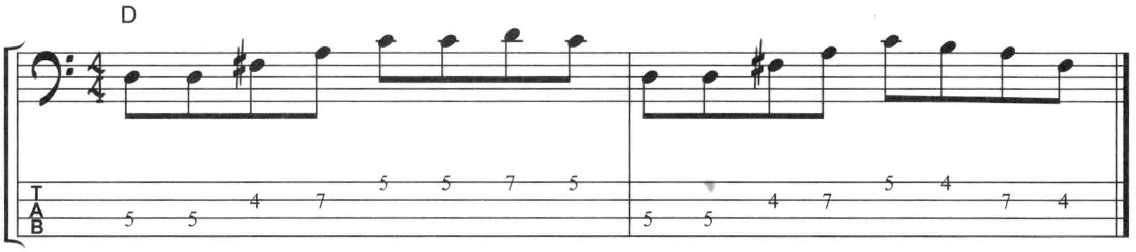

Also typical of many New Orleans tunes, Twist Ex. 6 is a simpler root-5 pattern that leaves more space but locks in nicely with the kick drum.

Twist Ex. 6

TRACK 24

The twist is a fun groove to play, and, considering how old it is, it's surprising how often it shows up on gigs. If you're cruising late-night vintage TV, you'll hear this time-tested feel on the theme songs to *The Munsters* (the coolest Twist ever!), *Peter Gunn*, and *Hawaii Five-0*—book 'em, Dano!

Twist Drum Key

The Motown Beat

Through the tireless efforts of Allan "Dr. Licks" Slutsky, the world has become familiar with James Jamerson, the legendary studio bassist who created a technical and musical revolution on the electric bass. Recording for the Detroit-based Motown record label, Jamerson played hit songs that became the soundtrack of life from the '60s to the present. While the Motown stylistic palette is varied and rich, one particular feel is immediately recognized as the "Motown groove." The snare-drum-banging-out-quarter-notes beat has fueled some of the biggest hit records of all time; Stevie Wonder's "Uptight (Everything's Alright)," Martha & the Vandellas' "Nowhere to Run," and the Four Top's "Reach Out (I'll Be There)" are three that come to mind. Motown Ex. 1 shows you the classic drum part. Amazingly simple, it's been the foundation for some of the most virtuosic bass lines ever played.

Motown Ex. 2 is one possible approach for this feel. This classic R&B pattern uses the major pentatonic scale to create a return to the root. It's similar to the Four Tops' "I Can't Help Myself (Sugar Pie Honey Bunch)."

Motown Ex. 1

TRACK 25

Motown Ex. 2

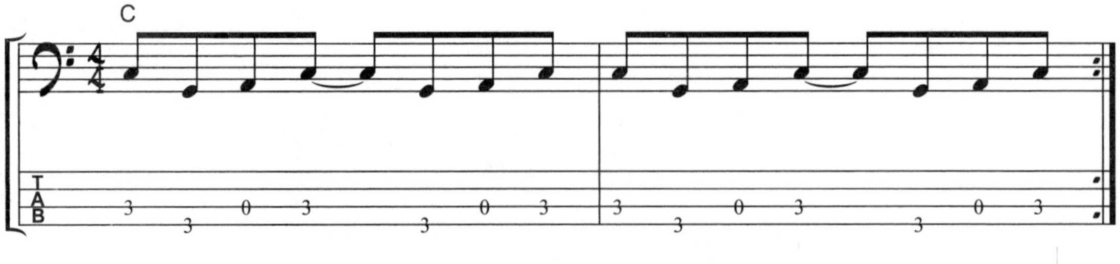

Motown Ex. 3 is a simple root–5 pattern that is extremely funky. Motown Ex. 4 is a time-honored bass rhythm that works in almost any style of music. Notice the hard-driving feel it creates when played with the Motown beat.

Motown Ex. 5 is a syncopated line that drops down to the lower 3rd of the chord and use a chromatic walk-up back to the root—another R&B stylistic hallmark. These examples will give you a basic sense of where to start if asked to create a Motown feel. Naturally the chord progression and a tune's specific rhythmic activity will further inform your choices.

Motown Ex. 3

TRACK 25

Motown Ex. 4

TRACK 25

Motown Ex. 5

TRACK 25

Motown Drum Key

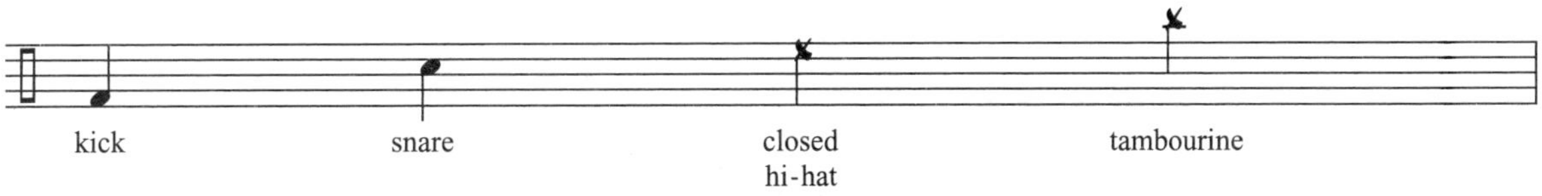

As an electric bassist, you have a sacred responsibility to dive into the recorded works of James Jamerson—the man who single-handedly changed the way the instrument is played and in turn changed the face of modern music and culture. A good place to start is the incomparable documentary *Standing in the Shadows of Motown*. The film tells the story of Jamerson and his fellow Funk Brothers, a group of studio musicians who played on the classic Motown hits. Next, buy Dr. Licks' now-classic book, *Standing*

in the Shadows of Motown: The Life and Music of Legendary Bassist James Jamerson* [Hal Leonard]. A wonderful telling of Jamerson's story as well as a treasure trove of transcriptions, it's a must-have for any electric bassist regardless of stylistic preference. The next step is to get your hands on the actual music; Motown collections are easy to find and generally inexpensive. Behind the landmark pop music craftsmanship, you'll hear and feel the sound of James Jamerson and the Funk Brothers locking in to the Motown groove.

Rock Steady

Let's talk about rock steady—not the famous Aretha Franklin tune of the same name (though Chuck Rainey's bass line is a great one to study)—we're talking about classic "rock steady" grooves of Jamaican pop music. Occurring roughly between 1966 and '68, the rock steady period saw the bass begin to dominate Jamaican music. Amid the new worldwide prominence of the electric bass, rock steady gave us some of reggae's most enduring bass "riddims."

Reggae is a broad genre with many stylistic subsets—each loaded with its own nuances—yet "reggae" has become a generic term for any music coming from Jamaica. Often on a gig someone will call a tune and say, "Play it reggae." What to play? A common misconception of reggae bass is, "Just don't play on beat *one*." Yes, some classic reggae lines skip the downbeat, but there are many more that lay into a big, fat *one*.

TRACK 26

Rock Steady Ex. 1

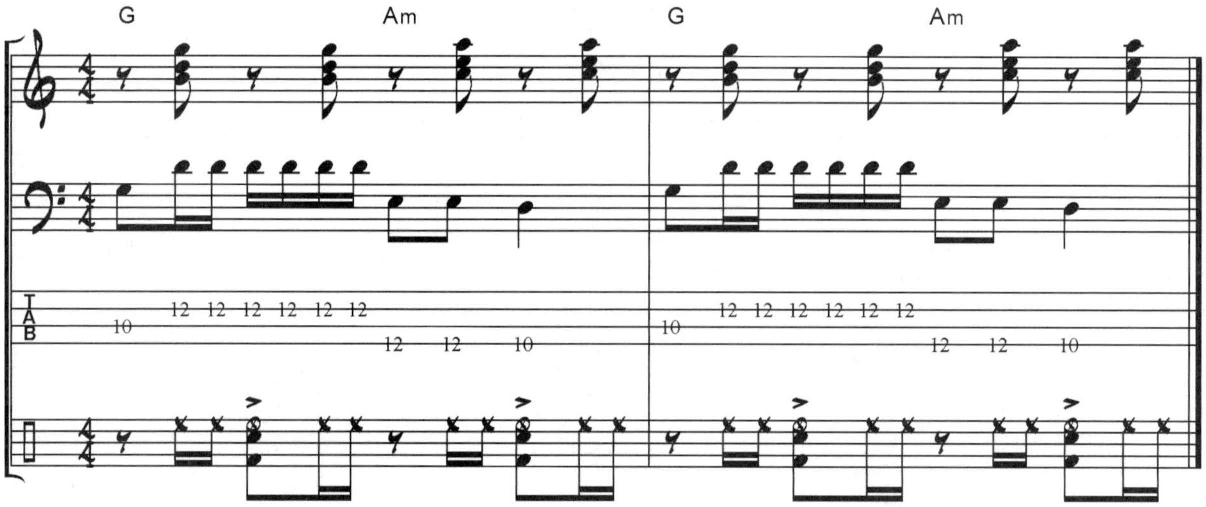

A common practice in Jamaican music is to reuse the bass line from a previous hit to make new hits. This tradition of "versioning" established certain lines as classics that apply to several titles. Rock Steady Ex. 1 is a typical pattern that jumps off the root and plays multiple repeats on the 5. It creates an incessant throb, especially when you dial in a lush reggae tone: Boost the lows, cut the highs, and hope your speakers can handle the bottom—no tweeters need apply! Play this line starting on the *A* string's 10th fret—the tone up there is fat and boomy. Slack off a bit on your 16th-note articulation. This isn't supposed to sound like Jaco; it's a lazy feel that was originally accomplished through the inhalation of *ganja* rolled up in the Sunday newspaper. The ideal tempo is around 82 BPM. The drum part leaves off the downbeat and lays heavily on the backbeats. This feel is sometimes referred to as the "one drop." To loosen it up, try throwing a 58% swing factor on your drum machine's 16th-notes, and use dynamics to let the hi-hat trail off on the pattern's last few notes. Also try a cross-stick instead of a snare drum sound. I've included the guitar/piano part, a simple upbeat emphasis known as the "skank."

Rock Steady Ex. 2 uses the repeating note again. Pound the root three times and then move up to the ♭7. The active guitar part gives the feel a new rhythmic dimension. The drum part is the same as in Ex. 1; play it around 75 BPM. Rock Steady Ex. 3 uses another repeating root motif; the drum part and the skank are the same as Ex. 2. The ideal tempo is around 84 BPM.

Rock Steady Ex. 2

TRACK 26

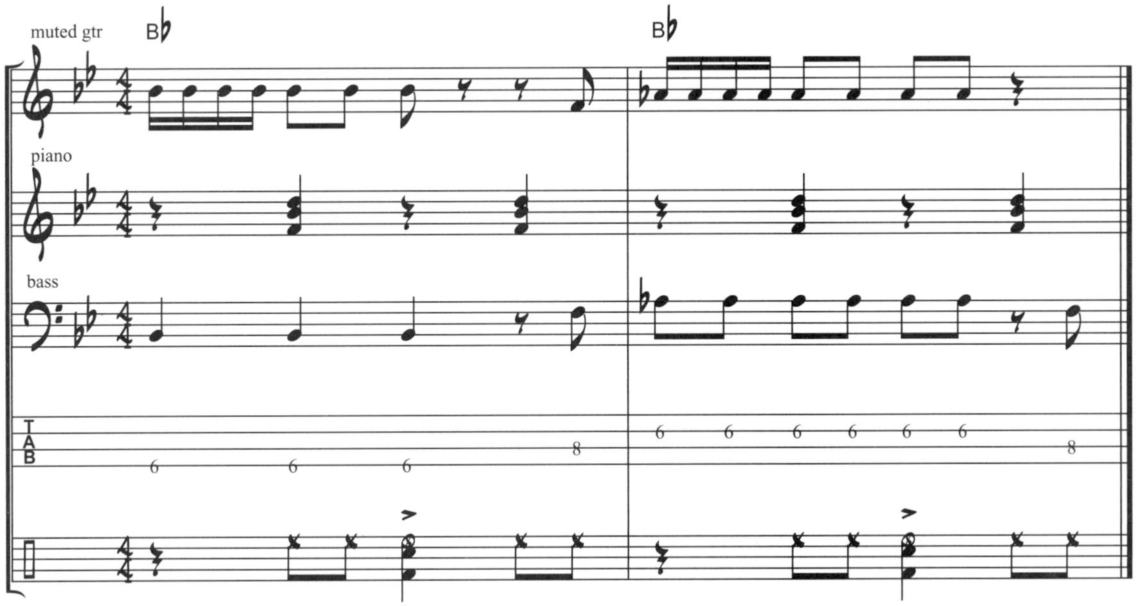

As you can see, these lines share many similarities, yet they are all different—and they all have a downbeat. You can adapt any of these patterns to songs to make them "reggae." Note, however, that another reggae characteristic is one- or two-chord vamps, so it gets tricky when you use bass patterns like these throughout a song with a lot of chords. But it can be done.

TRACK 26 **Rock Steady Ex. 3**

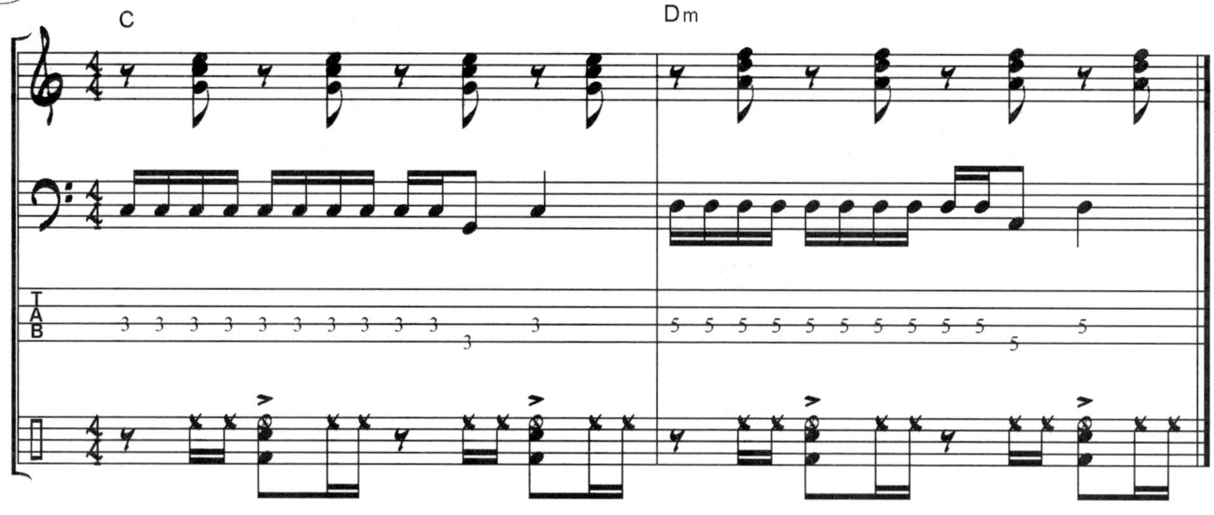

The Disco Octave Lick

The '70s brought many significant changes in popular music, including the emergence of disco. Like many innovations, disco music caused a clamorous rift, polarizing the music world into "disco lives!" and "disco sucks!" factions—a commotion the likes of which hadn't been seen since Beethoven broke away from the sonata-allegro form. Those who embraced the offbeat open hi-hat reveled in the shaking of their booties and found true enlightenment in disco's profound message. Yes, it was time to boogie-oogie-oogie till you just couldn't boogie no mo'. Those who spurned the four-on-the-floor kick drum found their own alternative styles, turning to the anger-fueled noise-fest that was punk rock. Still others rejected any shred of popularity and danced (in 11/8) to jazz fusion's compound meters, which deliberately obscured the downbeat until there was no hope of anyone shaking their groove things.

Those of us old enough to have gigged in the '70s remember the first time we were confronted with the disco octave tick. Many had a quizzical, amazed feeling of "that's it?" when we learned our task for the song. Others greeted this new convention with an enthusiastic sense of having found their calling, saying, "That's it!" Love it or hate it, if you are a working bass player, at some point you will have to make peace with the DOL.

To begin, program your drum machine to the classic disco beat (Disco Ex. 1). Many believe the drum machine was invented solely to relieve human beings (and drummers!) from the tedium of repeating this groove long enough to fill a 12" dance single.

Disco Ex. 1

Disco Ex. 2

TRACK 27

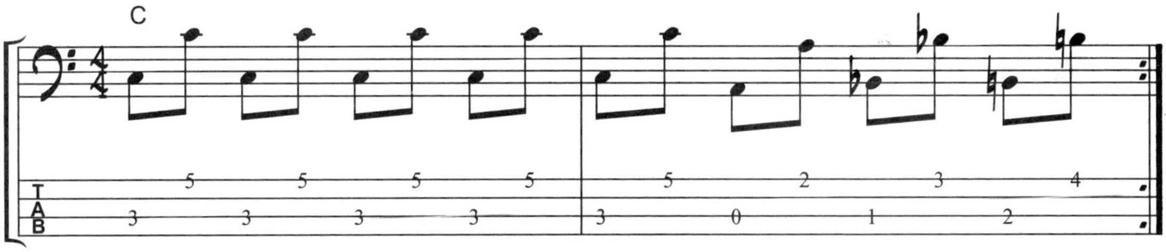

Disco Ex. 2 is the classic DOL, a vamp on a chord with straight up-and-down octaves. You can place the turnaround (the chromatic return from scale degree 6) every two or four bars depending on how disco-licious you feel. As simple as this may seem, it's challenging to get the octaves clean and consistent. Practice this slowly as a string-crossing exercise, alternating between your plucking-hand index and middle fingers. You might assign your index finger to the root and the middle to the octave. Another approach is to play the root with your thumb and the octave with your index finger; this makes the string-crossing easier, but it's harder to get consistent timbre and volume.

Disco Ex. 3 is another typical disco turnaround. It moves up to the minor 3rd before dropping down and returning to the root from the 6th. Disco Ex. 4 is a much-used DOL variation that breaks up the upbeat with two 16th-notes on the octave. Considering that disco is usually played in the 110–140 BPM range, this lick can be a real challenge to play

Disco Ex. 3

TRACK 27

Disco Ex. 4

TRACK 27

evenly. The 16ths need to be consistent—don't rush into them. As always, practice slowly to get it solid. This pattern has vexed many a bass player during the 20-minute Donna Summer medley. My favorite personal experience with this lick happened in 1979 when I was backing up Tiny Tim while he writhed his way through Rod Stewart's "Do Ya Think I'm Sexy?" The henna-haired crooner rolled on the floor yelping "reach out!" while the band mercilessly vamped on this lick for what seemed an eternity. All the while I was thinking, "Must . . . keep . . . 16th-notes . . . consistent . . . must . . . keep . . . "

Now that you've studied this paragon of modern musical innovation, it's time for you, brave bassist, to venture forth and create your own disco memories. Thanks to the geniuses of the advertising world (and the purveyors of pop culture), you can rest assured that the '70s and disco music will never go out of style. So lace up those mile-high platform shoes and catch the next bus to Funkytown.

Bom Bom

The title of this groove may lead you to think we are exploring an exotic form of sacred rainforest folk music: "The indigenous peoples of the Brazilian interior used *bom bom* as an accompaniment to rituals in which the worst drummer of the tribe would be sacrificed to appease the gods of time and rhythm." No such luck. "Bom bom" is the easiest way to describe what this groove sounds like: "Uh, dude . . . just go, 'bom bom.'" Two eighth-notes on the downbeat and voilà—bom bom. What's so special about that? Well, it's amazingly simple to do, and it works with a variety of drum grooves. Sometimes leaving a lot of space in your bass line is a beautiful thing. Hitting the eighth-notes on beat *one* sets up a feel for the rest of the bar, but you don't have to play anything else. That's why there are other musicians in the band.

Bom Bom Ex. 1 is the classic bom-bom groove, with a straightforward eighth-note-on-the-hi-hat underneath. Program it into your drum machine and play it for a while. Just be one with the simplicity—listen deeply and imagine all the amazing things that could come after you go "bom bom." Stick with that for a minute or two, and then give in to the temptation to fill up the space.

TRACK 28

Bom Bom Ex. 1

Now for some variations. For Bom Bom Ex. 2 I've expanded the drum part into the once-again-popular "vinny-boom-batz" groove. [See page 82.] Listen to the cumulative rhythm of the drum part: It's saying "boom-boom-batz, vinny-vinny-boom-batz." To nail this groove, set the drum machine's 16th-note swing factor between 58% and 62%. This groove has been co-opted by both the alt/indie/pop crowd and the hip-hop scene.

Bom Bom Ex. 2

TRACK 28

Bom Bom Ex. 3 is the dreaded "double bom bom—go "bom bom" on *one* and *three.* This creates a great '60s R&B/pop feel; use the swing factor again and you've got a groove similar to Aretha Franklin's "Baby I Love You." Try adding a subtle 16th-note pickup to beat *three*. Bom Bom Ex. 4 is a classic heavy-rock "C'mon, Sche-nectady—put your hands in the air!" groove. Similar to Queen's "We Will Rock You," this pattern is sure to rouse the fans. See if you can perfect the tricky move of thrusting your clenched right fist into the air on the backbeats.

Bom Bom Ex. 5 is the "Afro bom bom." The drums play an active Afro-Latin–tinged beat, and the bass goes "bom bom." This groove is reminiscent of the intro to Gladys Knight & the Pips' version of "I Heard It Through the Grapevine." James Jamerson used this rhythm to create a hypnotic, pulsating groove.

Bom Bom Ex. 3

TRACK 28

TRACK 28

Bom Bom Ex. 4

TRACK 28

Bom Bom Ex. 5

Bom Bom Drum Key

There are lots of other variations to try with this pattern—bom bom works with just about anything. Next time you practice with your band or jam with your friends, try it out and see what develops. This groove is easy; it doesn't require much from you, but that's a good thing. Bassists too often look for ways to plug up every hole in the music, and the result can be a jumbled mess. When everyone in the band competes for the space in a measure, no one wins. If we accept that 97% of the time the bassist needs to play on the downbeat, why not leave it at that and see how things open up?

The Meters—New Orleans Funk

There was a time when the music industry was less centralized. Independent record companies produced hits on their home turf, using local heavyweights for their house bands. If you were hip enough you could tell where a song was recorded just by listening closely to its groove and sound. Each region produced tracks with its own flavor, which was a product of the studio, the producers, and most important, the individual musicians who contributed their talents.

New Orleans has long been a hub of musical activity, with a distinctive sound and groove. There you can find a playing style best described as "laid back." Compared to Motown's more aggressive musicians, New Orleans players sound so laid back they seem to be falling off the backs of their chairs. Perhaps it's the 90-degree heat combined with 90% humidity—whatever, if you want to cop the N'awlins groove, y'all got ta relax!

The Meters were a group of Crescent City studio aces that backed Paul McCartney, Robert Palmer, Dr. John, LaBelle, Lee Dorsey, Allen Toussaint, Earl King, and countless other acts. In their spare time they recorded instrumental R&B classics like "Cissy Strut," "Funky Miracle," "Look-Ka Py Py," and "Pungee." Organist Art Neville, guitarist Leo Nocentelli, and legendary drummer Joseph "Zigaboo" Modeliste all had unique approaches to their instruments, but bass man George Porter Jr. created the honey-thick glue that held it all together. Still active, Porter has released solo records, and he tours with a revamped version of the band known as the Funky Meters.

The magic of the early Meters recordings is largely due to the symbiotic groove-match of Porter and Modeliste. Ziggy's playing can be compared to that of Tower Of Power's David Garibaldi, but slowed down to half speed and very greasy—he's active, loose, unpredictable, and undeniably funky. Porter plays the straight man much of the time, but he has the chops to bust out with intricate lines and fills when the spirit moves him. Porter's ability to play fat, solid lines anchors the music, making it impossible for the listener to sit still.

Meters Ex. 1 is a laid-back groove similar to the "Cissy Strut" solo section. Porter lets the music settle in for a nice ride by laying down big, fat notes with funky pickups. Notice how the octave on *three* creates a "flipped over" feel. The drum part is fairly complex, the feel being somewhere between straight and swing. To get close to the original groove, quantize your drum machine to 16th-note triplets. Pay careful attention to the dynamics in the hi-hat and kick-drum parts. Meters Ex. 2 is a busy, syncopated line in the style of "Pungee." The drums and bass are both goin' for it on this one. The kick and snare create a two-way conversation, and yet the bass line lays perfectly over the top. Watch the dynamics on the kick drum!

Meters Ex. 1

TRACK 29

TRACK 29

Meters Ex. 2

Meters Ex. 3 is a killer groove in the style of "Yeah, You're Right." The bass line is an easy syncopated lick that descends the pentatonic scale—but the drum part is insane. The kick drum practically takes over, but, in context, it supports the groove and sounds great. Program this beat slowly; the kick drum dynamics are crucial to achieving the right feel. Modeliste's drumming is organic and his grooves all vary over time, but these examples will give you a basic concept of what he plays. It's tough to make a drum machine sound like Ziggy. Listen to him and develop a sense of his dynamics and swing feel.

Make it a point to dig into the music of these groove masters; there are many compilations featuring their classic tracks. Two comprehensive collections are *The Meters Anthology: The Josie Years* [Repertoire] and *Funkify Your Life: The Meters Anthology* [Rhino].

TRACK 29

Meters Ex. 3

Soca

It's time to take a vacation (paid, of course!). This year we're checking into Club Ed, a posh, all-inclusive Caribbean resort that caters to low-frequency dwellers. Amenities include a 24-hour all-you-can-groove buffet; big, cushioned lounges that lay all the way back; a bubbling fountain of 16th-note finger-funk; and deep-blue water with churning triplet undercurrents. Best of all, you never have to bear a long, self-indulgent guitar solo, ever. The house band at Club Ed specializes in a musical style called soca.

The word "soca" combines "soul" and "calypso." Calypso music originated on the island of Trinidad and typically features lyrics drenched in political satire. Its musical influence can be felt all throughout the Caribbean islands, blending into styles such as reggae, merengue, Afro-Cuban, mento, and junkanoo. Soca was born when calypso musicians first heard the rhythmic drive of American soul music. In return, soca influenced American R&B and dance music with the unrelenting hi-hat rhythms that would fuel the disco craze. If you can get past the overheated histrionics of Buster Poindexter's 1987 version of "Hot Hot Hot," trace the tune back to soca star Arrow's original 1983 version—you'll hear soca music in its natural state.

Soca music is similar to other Afro-Caribbean styles in that the downbeat is not always accentuated. It's also typically felt in half-time. Most soca tunes revolve around a two-chord vamp: either V–I or I–V. Soca is primarily dance music, so play all of these examples at half-note equals 120 BPM. Soca Ex. 1's line looks simple but can be tricky to play. The lack of a downbeat takes some getting used to; try moving part of your body (preferably below the waist) to fill in the missing beats. The line uses the triad's 3rd and 5th degrees but leaves out the root, which is only occasionally filled in with an eighth-note pickup.

Soca Ex. 2 uses the same drum pattern (as do all of these examples) but has straightforward half-notes in the bass part. Laying back on the second half-note provides the characteristic lazy feel of island music. The fat, pumping half-note rhythm is the same as a merengue bass line. Soca Ex. 3 is a much more active line; it's easy to hear the influence of funk and R&B in this one.

Soca Ex. 1

TRACK 30

TRACK 30

Soca Ex. 2

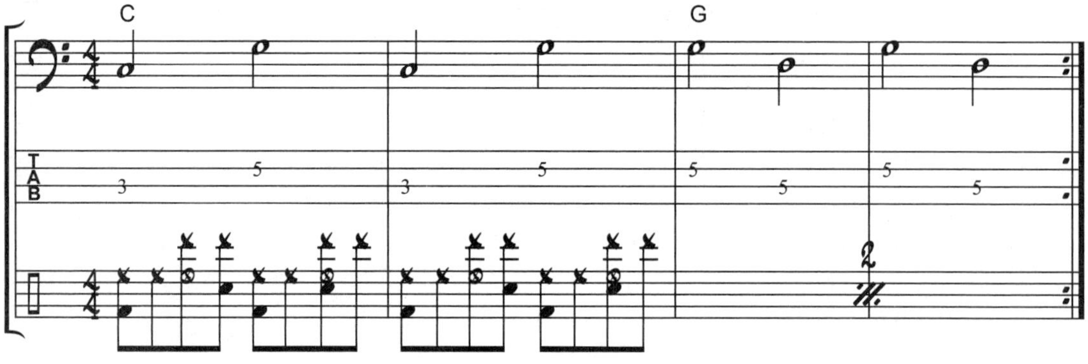

TRACK 30

Soca Ex. 3

Soca Ex. 4 uses an inverted arpeggio on the first chord, another typical soca device, while Soca Ex. 5 shows how to add some slap to the soca groove. In general, Afro-Caribbean music is ripe for slapping; there's always plenty of space to add percussive effects. Just don't step all over the steel drummer, or you may have to duck a flying pan!

Soca is definitely party music. The pulsating beat is irresistible, and the bass lines' unique rhythmic patterns are a blast to play. Have fun, mon!

Soca Ex. 4

TRACK 30

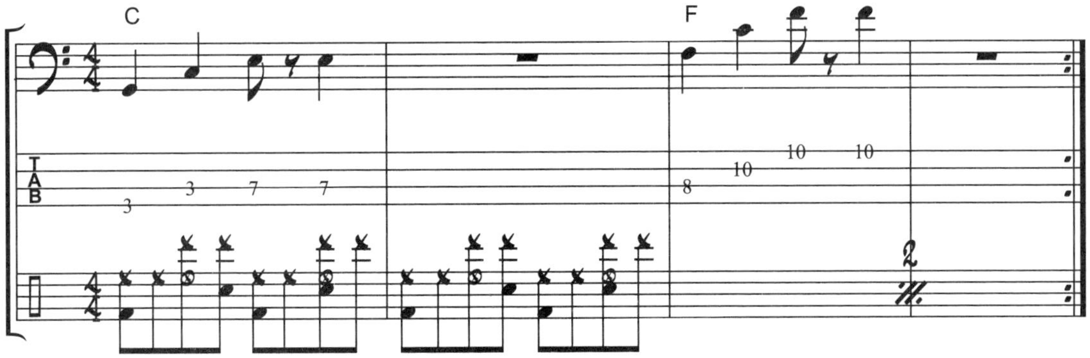

Soca Ex. 5

TRACK 30

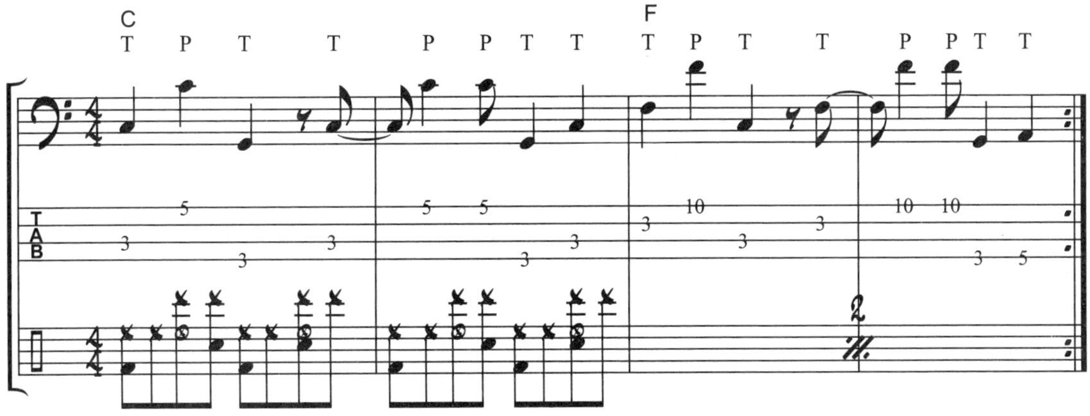

The Jimmy Reed Groove

Let's look at a classic blues groove that gets played all the time: the Jimmy Reed feel. Jimmy Reed was a major artist in Chicago's post-war blues scene, singing, playing guitar, and blowing harmonica on numerous hits for the Vee-Jay label. Many of his greatest tunes have become blues standards: "Big Boss Man," "Shame, Shame, Shame," "Bright Lights, Big City," and "Baby, What You Want Me to Do." Jimmy captured the 1950s R&B audience with his laid-back and folksy style, hitting No. 5 on the Billboard charts with "You Don't Have to Go."

While Reed's music encompasses several different feels, he is best known for the groove you can hear on "Big Boss Man." It shuffles, but it's not really a shuffle in the classic sense. The rhythm is essentially eighth-notes, but the length of the eighths is critical to the feel: The first eighth is short, the second long. Reed Ex. 1 shows the simple drum beat for this groove; it's a straight *one–three* kick drum, *two–four* snare with a swing pattern on the closed hi-hat. I've included the guitar part—it's an important piece of this groove.

Reed Ex. 1

You can approach this groove in a few ways, the simplest being Reed Ex. 2. Stay on the root and play the Jimmy Reed rhythm. Reed Ex. 3 is a slight variation, adding a little movement on beat *four*; make sure the 16th-notes swing. Reed Ex. 4 varies the line by using a classic major-triad pattern with a fill on beat *four*.

TRACK 31

Reed Ex. 2

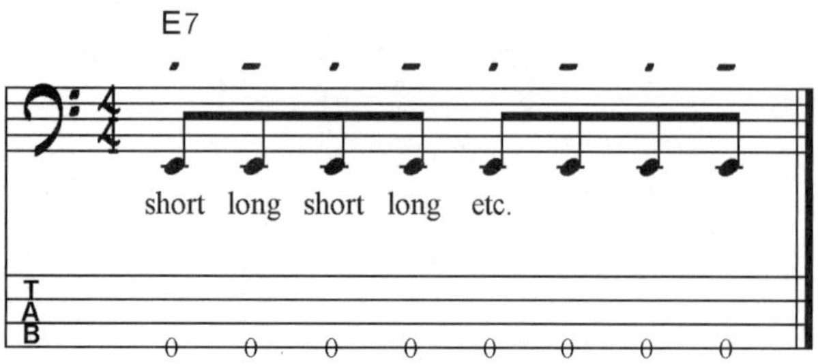

Reed Ex. 3

Reed Ex. 4

TRACK 31

Play these basic lines over the 12-bar blues form and you'll have the entire picture (Reed Ex. 5). Look closely at bars 11 and 12; this is the typical turnaround for this blues feel, especially bar 12's rhythmic kick on the V chord.

Have fun with this groove—it's a classic. Next time you're on a pickup blues gig, you can bet someone will call "Jimmy Reed in *E*."

Reed Ex. 5

TRACK 31

Vinny-Boom-Batz

Here's a cool retro groove that has made its way back into the pop consciousness via the '80s and '90s sampling craze. Hip-hop and rap producers were some of the first to embrace the concept of stealing—uh, I mean, sampling—an old groove and making it the basis of a new tune. Many of the resulting songs were based on '60s drum breaks, which are now widely available as loops on sample CDs as well as in drum machines and groove boxes. One such funky groove of yesteryear is called "vinny-boom-batz"—a.k.a. the Karen Carpenter groove. (Those of you old enough to remember watching her thrub the tubs will know what I mean.) This groove is all over the radio in styles ranging from hip-hop to alt-folk. It seems everyone loves Vinny.

Vinny Ex. 1 is the basic drum beat. Program the kick and snare dynamics to avoid sounding like a bad junior high stage-band drummer (though that has its own charm). The snare hits on the "a" of *two* and the "e" of *three* are much softer, almost ghosted. The kick-drum hits on the "and" of *two* and downbeat of *three* are also softer; you can even build in a slight crescendo to the "and" of *three*. Also, experiment with different degrees of swing; 58%–67% for the 16th-notes is a good range. Any more than that will make the feel sound choppy. Check out the subtle differences in the groove with and without the swing factor—swing gives the pattern a totally different vibe. The tempo can range from 70 BPM to 130 BPM.

Vinny Ex. 1

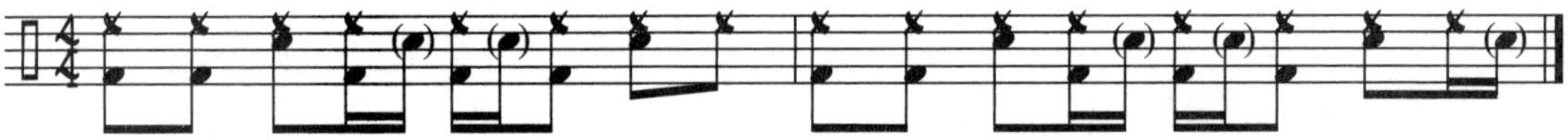

Bass lines that go with this groove can vary from a simple "bom bom" to something very active. Vinny Ex. 2 is a basic line that fits nicely and leaves plenty of room; it's classic Old School R&B in the vein of the Meters. Vinny Ex. 3 is the same idea but a little more active.

TRACK 32

Vinny Ex. 2

Vinny Ex. 3

TRACK 32

Vinny Ex. 4 is a simple line that uses a chromatic walk-up to the 5th; it's pure '60s (yeah, baby). Vinny Ex. 5 is a two-bar pattern that's busy—perhaps too busy. Reserve it for those moments when you're feeling way-out groovy and can't help but let your freak flag fly.

Vinny Ex. 4

TRACK 32

Vinny Ex. 5

TRACK 32

The "Green Onions" Groove

Let's look at another classic '60s R&B groove. The "Green Onions" groove takes its name from the 1962 Booker T. & the MG's hit of the same name. This quartet of studio aces acted as the house rhythm section for Memphis soul label Stax, backing Otis Redding, Wilson Pickett, Sam & Dave, Carla Thomas, and many others. Organist Booker T. Jones, bassist Donald "Duck" Dunn, drummer Al Jackson, and guitarist Steve Cropper propelled some of the '60s' biggest hits with their lean, cut-to-the-core grooves. (Although Duck Dunn is widely known for his role as the MG's anchor, he did not play on the classic "Green Onions" recording; original MG's bassist Lewis Steinberg laid down that line. Dunn didn't appear on an MG's record until 1965's *Soul Dressing*.) Along with Cropper, Duck Dunn ascended from studio obscurity to become a household name when both were featured players in the 1980 hit movie *The Blues Brothers*.

The "Green Onions" groove itself was first recorded by Sonny Boy Williamson as "Somebody Help Me." It is also recognizable as the basis for ZZ Top's "La Grange." The feel is essentially a shuffle, though not overtly. On the MG's recording, Jackson keeps a simple, straight-up-and-down beat with only a hint of swing on the ride cymbal. Onions Ex. 1 shows the original recording's bare-bones beat; it's a testament to the power of pure groove. In a perfect world, all drummers would groove this hard and show this much restraint! Onions Ex. 2 is a more active version of the drum groove, a standard shuffle.

Onions Ex. 3 shows the simple yet powerful bass line. The big push comes from the "skip" in the middle of beat *two*—make sure to leave the space between the triplet's first and third sub-beats, and give the third sub-beat a little accent to create some "top spin." It's possible to embellish this groove a little, but be careful—too much activity will ruin its natural beauty. Onions Ex. 4 shows a couple of ways to add to the line without destroying the groove; use them once in a while to mix it up.

TRACK 33

Onions Ex. 1

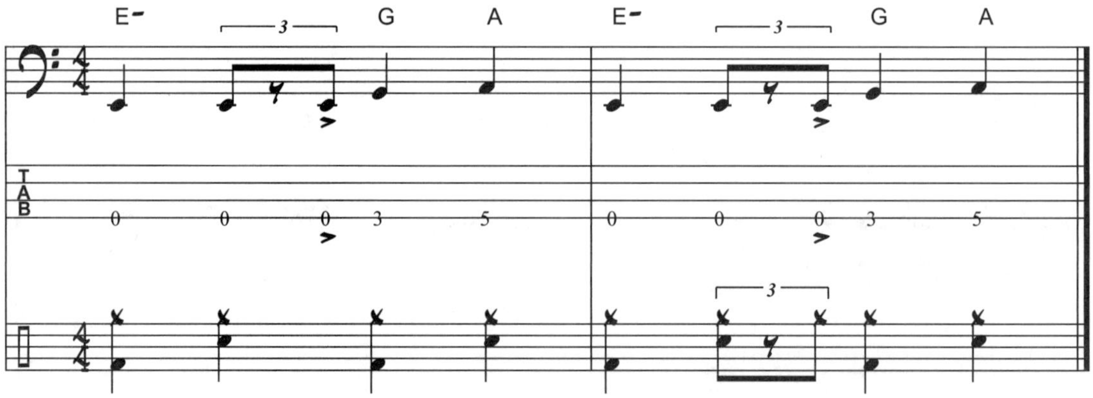

Onions Ex. 2

TRACK 33

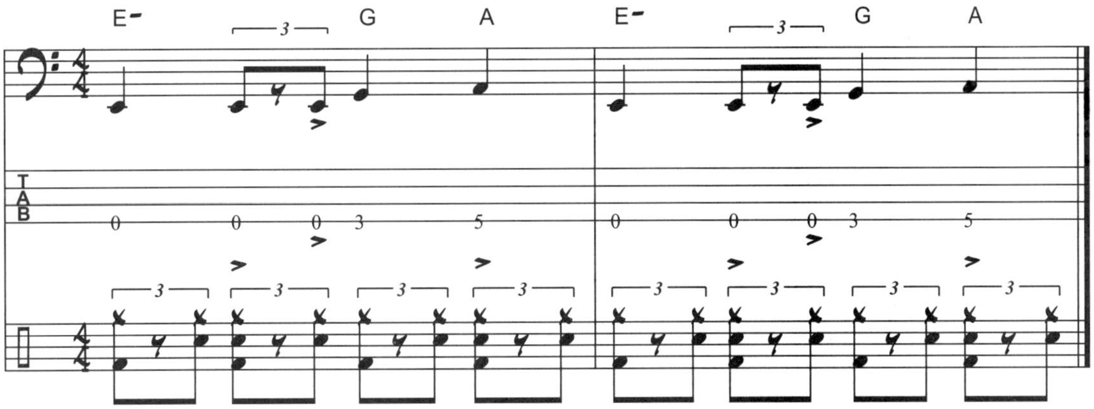

Onions Ex. 3

TRACK 33

Onions Ex. 4

TRACK 33

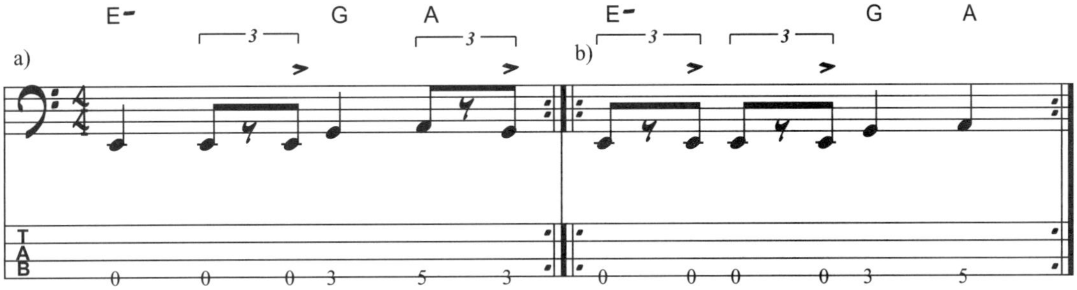

Onions Ex. 5 shows the line as it can be played through the 12-bar blues form. It has a definite minor quality, so if you want to play a fill, you can use minor-chord tones, minor-pentatonic scale tones, and the like. The line emphasizes a 1–♭3–4 pattern, so you can play major triads off the ♭3 and 4. Have fun with this time-honored bass line—it's a true classic.

TRACK 33

Onions Ex. 5

Cajun

Once again let's return to the fertile territory of Louisiana. I'm always amazed at how much incredible music is rooted there. Cajun music has enjoyed several popular revivals over the generations, thanks to artists like Hank Williams, Doug Kershaw, Beausoleil, and Dolly Parton. The Cajun folk tradition was brought to Louisiana by Acadians migrating from French Canada, so it's typically sung in the French dialect particular to this group. As with most folkloric music, it was created with whatever instruments were handy: guitars, fiddles, accordions (the push-button concertina type, not the big keyboard type), and maybe a bass—possibly of the washtub variety. For percussion they used anything they could bang on, most frequently the *frottoir*—or "rub board" (washboard)—tambourine, and a metal triangle big enough to call in the hogs from across the county line.

Contemporary Cajun music sounds a lot like country music. Cajun bands use much the same instrumentation as country groups, with the addition of the accordion. Country has in fact been a major influence on the style; think Hank Williams's classic "Jambalaya." Still, idiosyncrasies persist that are unique to Cajun music.

One thing about Cajun (as well as much other folk music) is the unusual phrase lengths. An eight-bar phrase is not always the standard; sometimes the phrase is extended at the end until the singer starts the next line. Often there are bars of 2/4 thrown in to extend one chord, or perhaps as a quick bounce to the V chord. Harmonically, traditional Cajun tends to be very simple: mostly I and V chords, and sometimes the IV for a little excitement. The trick is knowing when to change. Listening to the vocals is your best bet.

Cajun Ex. 1 is a classic Cajun waltz with a typical drum part. The bass line's quarter-note interpretation is unique: Beat *one* is played long, while *two* and *three* are kept short, but not too short. Chances are your drum machine does not have a washboard sound; the closest thing may be the guiro. That instrument is made of wood, not metal, but at least it produces sound the same way—the player rubs something over a corrugated surface. The triangle is not an uncommon drum-machine sound. If you have one, tune it down until it sounds like it has 12" sides made of wrought iron. A ride-cymbal bell will suffice in a pinch; tune it down just a tad, and if you can control the decay, shorten it a bit. Now you're cookin' with 'gator!

Cajun Ex. 1

TRACK 34

Cajun Ex. 2 is the waltz again, embellished a bit with triplet pickups. Beat *one* is long, while the other notes are short. Feel the little space between the triplet pickups, and "ghost" them a little. Bar 8 has a typical walk-up line to the top. It's fine to use even though the chord stays on C—hey, it's folk music! If you have a synth or soundcard and you really want to complete the groove, dial in an accordion patch and program the chord progression into a sequencer. Use the root on *one*, and then put a simple root–3–5 triad on *two* and *three*. How 'bout dat?

TRACK 34

Cajun Ex. 2

TRACK 34

Cajun Ex. 3

Cajun Ex. 3 is a two-step; it's pretty basic, except for where the chord changes occur. Bar 4's quarter-notes set up the V chord; play them short. Also notice how the walking fill starts in the middle of bar 7 and continues through bar 8. This helps make an unusual harmonic rhythm feel more natural. The 10-bar phrase is typical; it helps the progression feel settled.

Cajun Ex. 4 is a common Cajun chord progression. Starting on the IV chord, it has a circular nature that lends itself to long interpretations. Cajun music is frequently played to accompany dancing—in fact, you almost never see a Cajun band playing without dancing in the audience, planned or not. The infectious rhythms of the washboard and triangle—coupled with the prodding thump of oom-pah bass—make sitting still next to impossible.

Cajun Ex. 4

TRACK 34

Cajun Drum Key

Zydeco

Continuing our musical tour of Louisiana, let's look at zydeco, Cajun music's city cousin. Like Cajun, zydeco is rooted in the bayous of Louisiana, but it's also influenced by rock, R&B, and urban culture. Zydeco is a musical gumbo usually sung in Creole French, augmented with washboards and accordions—pretty cool stuff.

The acknowledged king of zydeco is Clifton Chenier, a Creole accordionist and singer from Opelousas, Louisiana. His early singles for the Specialty label were first compiled on the 1955 LP *Zodico Blues & Boogie*, but his recording career spanned several decades until his death in 1987. Another popular artist is Buckwheat Zydeco (born Stanley Dural), an accordionist considered heir to Chenier's throne. Coming from a funk background, Buckwheat expanded his group to include R&B-inspired horns. Buckwheat's longtime bassist, Lee Allen Zeno, is a groove monster; his bubbly, Jerry Jemmott–style 16th-notes have pushed zydeco into a whole new direction. Other notable zydeco artists include Zachary Richard, Boozoo Chavis, Nathan [Williams] & the Zydeco Cha Chas, C.J. Chenier, and Queen Ida, whose bassist, Terry Buddingh, is *Bass Player* magazine's contributing Technical Editor.

As Terry explains: "Zydeco is primarily dance music, and you can see something special happen when the dancers are really feeling the groove. I try to emulate their groove with my playing. That's what it's all about—laying down a big groove until the place busts open from the ecstatic energy. In Louisiana people expect to see the band bustin' ass; no sandbagging is allowed. The bass has to have a lot of energy—it's perhaps the most important element in establishing the zydeco feel. The tone should be as punchy as possible; you're not only driving the band, you're also driving the entire dance floor.

"While zydeco has many varieties, the two-chord, eight-bar vamp is probably the most common basis for a tune: four bars of I, two bars of V, and two bars of I, played in a 2/4 half-note feel and boosted with energized fills. Queen Ida's 'Hey la Bas' and Rockin' Sidney's 'My Toot Toot' are classic tracks with this feel."

Zydeco Ex. 1 shows an approach for this vamp. Keep the pickup notes short. On your drum machine, use sounds similar to those you used with Cajun music: your short and long guiro sounds can substitute for the washboard. Tune up the long guiro so it's close in pitch to the short guiro.

Terry continues: "There's also a more energized 4/4 style that a lot of hardcore zydeco bassists are playing. Built on a spiced-up boogie-woogie walking bass line, the 'double-pump' kick-drum feel is very popular; Nathan & the Zydeco Cha Chas play this groove all night long, and the dancers love it. It's the younger generation's zydeco; it has plenty of soul, but it's higher-energy and not so primitive." Ex. 2 shows the classic "double-pump" groove with a more active bass line built from the major pentatonic scale. On your drum machine, adding 58% swing to the eighth-notes will give the groove a different character.

Another staple of the zydeco diet is the shuffle. With their high-energy approach, zydeco shuffles are much faster than your typical Chicago or Texas shuffle. Zydeco Ex. 3 shows two variations for the drum part. The first is a typical "double-stroke" shuffle on the snare; the second is a "flat tire" feel with the snare playing just the last triplet of each beat. Again, the bass line is built from the major pentatonic scale.

Zydeco Ex. 1

TRACK 35

Zydeco Ex. 2

TRACK 35

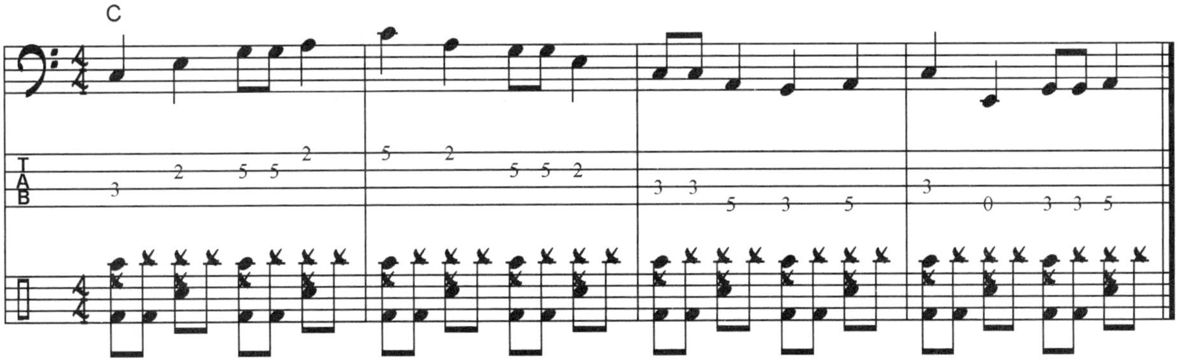

"It's important to know that there are essentially two approaches to zydeco," notes Terry. "Most bands that play around Louisiana are basically dance bands; they play two-steps, shuffles, and waltzes, and the people come primarily to dance. Bands that travel more, like Queen Ida, Buckwheat, and Terrance Simien, have a broader approach and incorporate a wider variety of influences to appeal to a more diverse audience. You'll

TRACK 35

Zydeco Ex. 3

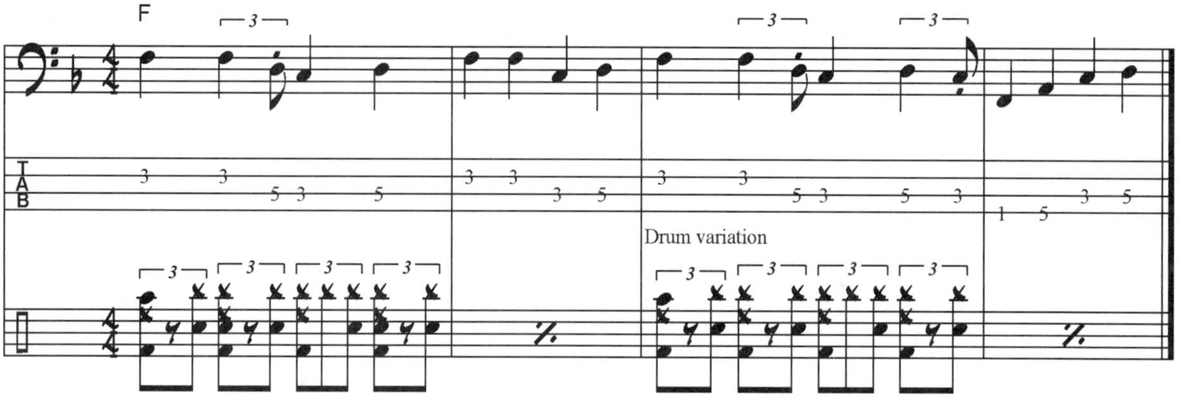

still hear dance tunes, but you'll also hear New Orleans R&B, Caribbean, blues, and other flavors mixed in. To keep a concert flowing and maintain interest, pacing and dynamics become more important, so variety is required."

On copping an authentic zydeco groove, Terry advises, "The trick is to visit southwest Louisiana and tune into the whole scene. Absorb the culture, eat some gumbo, get funky with a big plate of crawfish, check out the way people talk and the way they take their time doing the things they do—but dig how serious they become when it's time to party. Watch people who really know how to dance. The dances are about more than the music and dancing—there's a cultural thing going on that connects with a deep and rich tradition. Try to emulate all of that when you play. Then you'll really be playing some zydeco."

There are many places to learn more about this exciting music style. Some links Terry suggests are www.louisianamusicfactory.com, nathanwilliams.crazygator.com, and www.swallowpublications.com.

Go-Go

Let's head to our nation's capital to check out an influential subgenre of funk. You might never guess it, but beyond the marbled entranceways and granite edifices of the uptight political mothership that is Washington, D.C., boils the bubbling cauldron of groove-aliciousness known as go-go music. Popularized in the 1980s by artists like Chuck Brown & the Soul Searchers, Trouble Funk, Rare Essence, and E.U., go-go was a bottom-oriented derivative of funk that featured a kick-drum-heavy mix, Latin percussion, and a good-time aesthetic. E.U.'s "Da Butt" is the most well-known go-go track; it hit big in '88 with an infectious groove, transparent sexuality, and freak-on-a-leash vocals. No big message here—ain't nothin' but a party.

One of the earliest instances of the go-go groove shows up in the '70s with Grover Washington Jr.'s soul-jazz classic, "Mr. Magic." While the smooth-as-silk performance is a far cry from go-go's raw energy, the main groove influenced much of what developed in the '80s. Go-Go Ex. 1 is the quintessential go-go groove—basically the "Mr. Magic" feel, but heavier. Like most go-go, this example has a swing undercurrent, so set your drum machine's quantization to 16th-note triplets. I've written the examples as straight 16ths to simplify programming and playing; interpret them with a swing feel and you're all set. I've also separated the percussion parts from the drum track to make this groove easier to read. Programming a realistic conga part is tricky; pay attention to the accents and dynamics to get close to the real deal. Notes in parentheses are quieter, while accented notes are louder. The conga part is written for the standard low and high conga sounds; if you have a more extensive set of tones available, experiment. Congas are a great texture to use on many different grooves, but they can sound stiff and sterile if you ignore dynamics. Pay attention to the markings, and see what other nuances you can create with your own touch sensitivity. The bass part doubles the kick drum; the space is important.

Go-Go Ex. 1

TRACK 36

If you want to funk it up a bit, add some well-placed dead notes and a little popped hammer-on in the classic spot, as in Go-Go Ex. 2. Go-Go Ex. 3 is similar to the groove on "Da Butt." On the original you'll hear the familiar crunch of a 1977 Fender Jazz Bass in the hands of Marcus Miller. To get the classic '80s vibe happening, pick a drum kit that has big, processed kick and snare sounds. The bass part is sparse; you can funk at will, or let it breathe with lots of space around the notes—whatever you think works for the moment.

Heralded as D.C.'s "King of Go-Go," Chuck Brown broke out in 1978 when "Bustin' Loose" scored four consecutive weeks at the top of the R&B charts. Though this seemed to signal the rise of go-go as a national trend, it never caught on nationwide. While hip-

TRACK 36

Go-Go Ex. 2

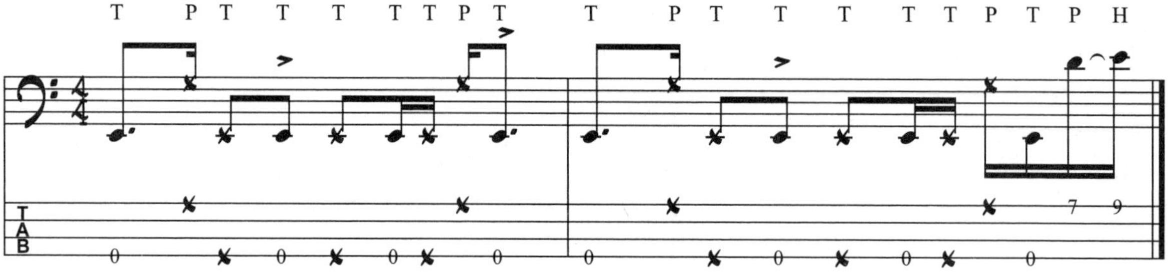

TRACK 36

Go-Go Ex. 3

hop forged ahead with the new technologies of sampling and drum machines, go-go was a more organic, human approach. Rather than rely on machines and stolen—I mean, sampled—riffs, go-go artists went in there and got their hands greasy with the essential oils of funk.

Brown dipped into the jazz pool with great frequency. His live shows were filled with go-go-ized covers of jazz standards such as "My Funny Valentine," "It Don't Mean a Thing If It Ain't Got That (Go-Go) Swing," and "Take the Go-Go Train." While funkifying jazz tunes was nothing new, a roomful of go-go partiers freakin' to Duke Ellington was something different. Chuck also recorded several slower R&B ballads, showing off his crooning abilities. But when it comes to go-go, hard-slammin' party funk is the order of the day. Here are a few classic Chuck Brown-inspired grooves.

Go-Go Ex. 4 is reminiscent of "Bustin' Loose." The bass line leaves lots of space, mainly hitting the accents with the kick drum. Fight the temptation to plug up every hole; let the groove breathe. Bass players are used to being involved with every beat of a tune, but in this case, don't mess with da funk—rests can be very groovy. This groove is a straight-16th feel, but try adding a 54% swing feel to the 16th-notes to loosen it up just a bit. The conga part is active; pay attention to the accents and ghosted notes, which play a big role in making this sound good. That goes for the hi-hat part, as well.

Go-Go Ex. 4

TRACK 36

Go-Go Ex. 5 is a swinging 16th-note feel that's similar to Chuck Brown's version of "My Funny Valentine" and is big in funk-jazz. Again, leave the holes in the groove open—sit with it and see how it feels to leave room for the band to lock in. However, you must perfectly nail your notes in order to set up the right feel during the rests. The drum part is written in straight 16ths; use a 62% swing factor on your drum program to get the right feel. The shaker part becomes a jazzy ride-cymbal–type pattern once you add the swing factor.

Go-Go Ex. 6 shows sample fills for the rest on beat *four*; some are more active than others. Set up the groove on your drum machine and practice different ways to fill. Remember, a fill should never interrupt the groove's flow—if it does, you've blown it. A favorite live-show shtick is to lock into a groove like this and let everyone else trade off on the fills. While it would seem that the flashiest, busiest fills would get the best response, often the bass player laying into a big, fat quarter-note on *four* wins the game by grooving harder than anyone else. Try it sometime!

TRACK 36

Go-Go Ex. 5

TRACK 36

Go-Go Ex. 6

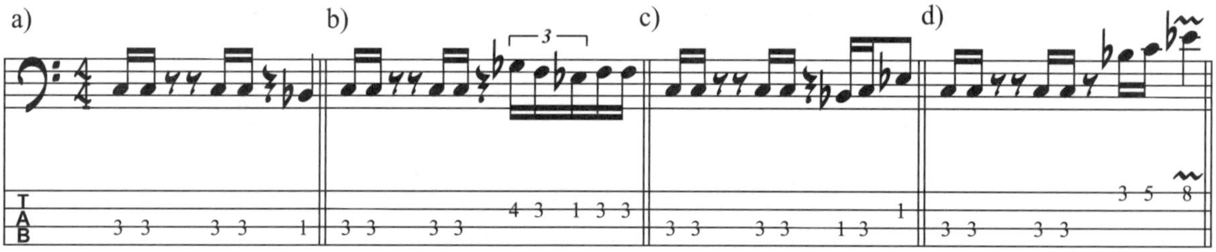

Go-go was an influential force in the hip-hop universe; check into the go-go artists I mentioned to get a better understanding of how they contributed to contemporary R&B. Have fun with these funky feels, and remember, in the words of Chuck Brown, "It don't mean a thing if it ain't got that go-go swing!"

Go-Go Drum Key

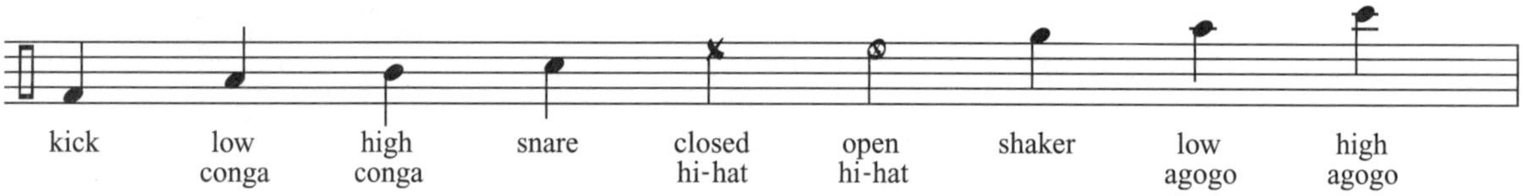

Chapter 4

THE PROS TALK GROOVE

When it comes to talking about the groove, you have to go to the source—the players who lay down some of the heaviest grooves on the planet. Each has a unique style, sound, and sense of where the groove is. As different as these players are, all agree the groove is about the feeling you create while you play. I asked each player the same questions:

> "The groove is the rhythmic motif of a song."
>
> —*Kim Stone*, *Spyro Gyra, the Rippingtons*

- How do you describe groove?
- How do you cultivate groove?
- Is there an activity or exercise you do to get in the groove?
- Is there a particular line or style that sums up where your groove comes from?
- Are there any special techniques you use to enhance the groove?

Phil Chen

Phil Chen

A native of Jamaica, Phil Chen was schooled by the masters of reggae. He has recorded with Rod Stewart, Jeff Beck, Pete Townshend, and Jackson Browne, among others, and in 2003 he toured with the re-formed Doors.

"Groove is intangible—it's a feel. When you play with other musicians, you don't need to talk, you play—you go to another plateau. It's important for me to find a drummer who understands what I'm doing without saying anything. I love playing with Richard Bailey; we grew up on the same island. When we play, we don't talk—we just enjoy.

"I like to practice a thing I call 'Engelbert Humperdink' with a chromatic scale [Pros Ex. 1]. I say the syllables while I play the line.

> "The groove is a living entity with all of the mystic attributes of life as we know it. It must be served and serviced."
>
> —*Jerry Jemmott, New York/ Muscle Shoals session bassist*

"If there's a section of a tune that I can't get right away, I take the line and make up lyrics that match the music; that way I can become one with it. When you have a musical sentence in your mind, you can play a part more convincingly. The rhythm I played on Rod Stewart's 'Do Ya Think I'm Sexy' or Jeff Beck's version of 'She's a Woman' is a good example of where my groove comes from—there was a tune popular in Jamaica called 'Poppa Top,' so I put it into the bass line: 'poppa-top, poppa-top, poppa-top . . .'

"When the groove isn't right, I listen to where the kick drum is and try to get as close as possible with that—I have to play as simple as possible and listen to everybody. When you play with everybody you become a team.

"I like to use open strings to make a line groove, like what James Jamerson does in 'I Was Made to Love Her.' Moving from the *D♭* to *E♭* triad, use an open instead of fingered *D* [Pros Ex. 2]. You have to play the open string with the same intensity as the other notes—it pushes the air; it breathes."

Pros Ex. 1

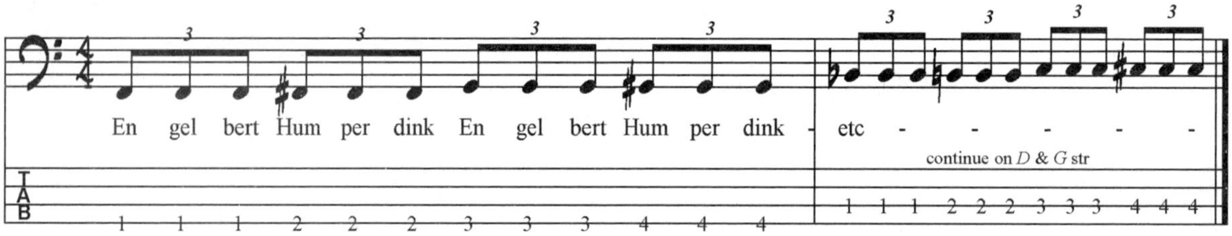

Pros Ex. 2

Harvey Brooks

Harvey Brooks can be heard on some of the most influential recordings of the '60s and '70s, including Bob Dylan's Highway 61 Revisited, *Miles Davis's* Bitches Brew, *and Al Kooper and Michael Bloomfield's* Super Session. *A member of the groundbreaking rock-blues band Electric Flag, he also recorded with the Doors, John Sebastian, Mama Cass, and many others.*

"Groove is when it feels right, when I'm locked with the drums. The groove has its own life. When you've eliminated all the things you don't need to play, the groove is communicated, which in turn makes everybody feel good. To cultivate the groove, I have to assess the overall vocabulary of what is being played and find the essence. Once I have that, it's a matter of adjusting to the breathing of the players. When I'm in the groove, it's a key going into a lock and all the tumblers falling into place.

"To get into the groove I need flexibility. I find that if I'm comfortable and loose, my groove is good. To get physically comfortable on the bass, I do a lot of chromatic things up and down the neck for about a half-hour before I play. If my mind is loose and my fingers are loose, my vocabulary flows and I can do what I can do. This exercise [Pros Ex. 3] really stretches out my hands. I start on the *G* string and play with fingers 1, 2, 3, and 4, then slide up one fret with the pinky. Then I come down 4, 3, 2, 1, slide up one fret on the 1st finger, and repeat the pattern up to the 12th fret. Then I head back down the neck. When I'm done with the *G* string, I repeat this on the *D*, *A*, and *E*. I use a quarter-note click and play eighths or 16ths against it."

Harvey Brooks

"My groove is coming from a New York '60s R&B/Wilson Pickett kind of flavor [Pros Ex. 4]. Some of the feel tips I got were from Eric Gale. He was a guitar player who played bass on a lot of recordings [Aretha Franklin, Bob James, Phil Upchurch]." The syllables in Pros Ex. 4 are the ones Harvey used to communicate the groove over the phone; notice how he fills in the rests with percussive sounds.

"Sometimes I use ghost-notes or palm-muted strings. These techniques give me rhythmic articulation without a defined pitch. There are no rules when it comes to the groove—you have to do whatever makes it work. You may have to play a groove you haven't experienced before, but you still need to make it solid and feel good, and make it sound like it's easy."

Pros Ex. 3

Pros Ex. 4

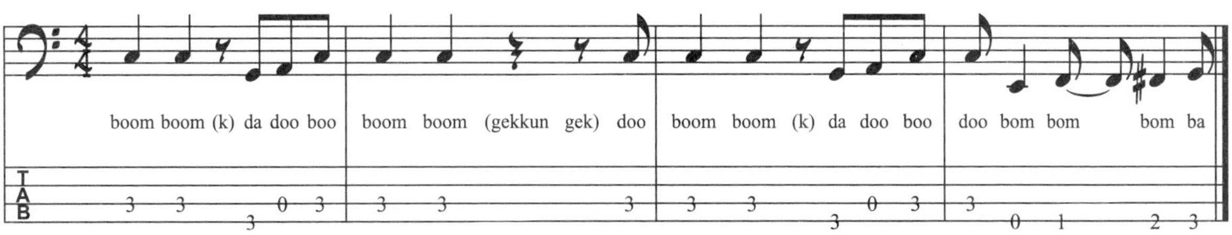

Hutch Hutchinson

Bonnie Raitt's longtime live and studio bassist, Hutch Hutchinson has also recorded with B.B. King, Ziggy Marley, Delbert McClinton, Randy Newman, Linda Ronstadt, and many others.

"Groove is an interaction between musicians, a pocket. Groove can be intense and deep or it can be light and lilting. Groove is the pulse that propels a tune, the heartbeat of music. Nothing functions without a groove.

"You can develop or cultivate the groove, but in a deeper sense it's something you inherently feel. If you have it, you can utilize it in all sorts of ways and different forms. In a group situation, the groove is somewhat situation-specific. If it's not coming together, you have to play less and give the drummer space to let the groove develop. On the other hand, sometimes you may have to assert yourself. If you have a definitive idea of how a tune is going to work—and you can express it—you should be as assertive as you can to make it happen. Sometimes a groove depends on the melody line, the phrasing of the singer, or lead instrumentalist. Focusing on the tune's melodic concept can really help you develop an idea for a pocket.

Hutch Hutchinson

"Play with other people and become versed in different styles—broaden your horizons. Check out types of music you might not otherwise listen to. It's important to be well versed, because these days so many different styles are blending together, not just in world music, but in pop music, too."

"I'm into the New Orleans vibe. Swamp funk and old-time jazz swing are what I grew up around, and I'm also heavily influenced by the Memphis guys like Tommy Cogbill and Duck Dunn, and by Jerry Jemmott, a New York player who worked a lot in Muscle Shoals. Those are the kinds of grooves I love to play and find second nature. This groove [Pros Ex. 5] is similar to what I play on Bonnie Raitt's 'Fool's Game' [on *Silver Lining*]. When I play it I sort of trance out with the piano and drums. My suggestion about how to hit this groove would be—eat a bunch of gumbo."

Pros Ex. 5

"The groove is that intangible thing that propels the music. The groove solidifies the pulse and makes the music have that infectious feeling that makes the listener want more. The groove is the responsibility of each individual in the group, and the bass player is the individual who anchors it. As a bassist, the ability to get, maintain, and sustain a groove is what people remember you by the most."

—*Rufus Reid, jazz artist, educator, and author*

Victor Bailey

Known as the player who took over Jaco Pastorius's Weather Report bass chair. Victor Bailey has also recorded with Michael Brecker, Mary J. Blige, Andy Summers, Steps Ahead, Ernie Watts, Lenny White, and many others. As a leader he has recorded Bottom's Up, Low Blow, *and* That's Right.

Victor Bailey

"Groove is a feeling that you give the music, whether it's swing or funk or whatever. As far as cultivating the groove, I guess it's just something I've always had. I started out playing funk and R&B—the music, the situations, and the people I played with were all about grooving. When I went into jazz, I took that with me. After Jaco came out, a lot of bassists forgot about the groove part of playing and became virtuoso lead players. I like the virtuoso thing when it's time for that, but when I'm playing with the band I always have to be locked in with the drummer and grooving.

"I've been very fortunate that since I was young I've always worked with people who emphasized the importance of groove. Particularly in Weather Report, as high a level of musicianship as that was, playing with Joe Zawinul the music had to always feel good. You could have all

Pros Ex. 6

> "Groove is difficult to describe to someone but undeniable to feel when you're in it. Whether you're the musician or the listener, there is simply no better musical connection to the human body than being locked in that pocket."
>
> *—Dave Ellefson, Megadeth*

the chops in the world, but if you're not grooving you won't last with him.

"To get in the groove, before I actually play anything I just try to feel it. In the studio I'll listen to the track and start to sing something to myself that's more of a feel, not even specific notes, like 'doom-doom, chick-um-da-doom-doom,' until I find something that works. Then I look for the notes. In some cases there may already be a specific line they want me to play, so I start singing the bass line before I play it and figure out what's going to make it groove. Is it on top of the beat or behind? Is this note longer or shorter? When I start to feel good singing it, I translate that to the instrument.

"The groove that really comes from me is a funky groove with a swing feel and a triplety undercurrent [Pros Ex. 6]. I'll do a two- or four-bar pattern and add little variations. I like to keep it subtle; I don't want to jump out and detract from the soloist. These are the kind of little things that won't get you voted Best Bassist, but will get you on a hundred more records than the guy who does."

Gary Grainger

As a member of John Scofield's band, Gary Grainger laid down some of the heaviest funk-jazz of the '90s. He has also recorded with artists such as Dennis Chambers, Nancy Wilson, and Ken Navarro. He and his brother, drummer Greg Grainger, have released Phase I *and* Phase II *as the band Grainger.*

Gary Grainger

"When I play in the rhythm section and all the things are hitting together, it creates that locking rhythm that makes you feel good, makes you want to move.

"When I was developing my groove, I would record myself when I practiced and listen back. Just like sequencing with computers, you can quantize differently, change the swing factor, choose different levels. By doing it yourself, in a human way, you learn to control where you put things.

"If the groove isn't happening, you can try to adjust to the person you're playing with—you can move over to their side and break it down and figure out what's wrong. You have to talk it out and see if you can make it work.

"It's important to warm up before you play. I do some stretches off the instrument, then maybe some scales up and down the neck. If my hands are loose, then everything works together, body and mind.

Pros Ex. 7

"Bassists need to recognize the different styles and what distinguishes them. R&B has a laid-back feel; Latin is different than a James Brown groove. One of my favorite feels is a funky Latin groove. I like to play a nice tight groove and play off the *one*. A track on Grainger *Phase II*, 'If You Were Mine,' fits that description [Pros Ex. 7].

"I use half-muting to help make a ballad groove; I picked that up from Anthony Jackson. It gives the bass a thick, warm sound with a softer attack that punches through the track. It all depends on the tune—you have to adjust how you play to suit the track."

Jack Casady

One of the pioneers of rock bass and a certified legend, Jack Casady was a founding member of the Jefferson Airplane and Hot Tuna, and he has recorded with artists such as Jimi Hendrix, David Crosby, Gov't Mule, and Warren Zevon.

Jack Casady

"Groove is the ability to communicate with the meter of a song. It's a heartfelt feeling that gives you the pulse regardless of what else is going on. It's not just about repeating a lick over and over, it's feeling the music and communicating with the people you're playing with. As a bassist you have to listen to everyone else and allow yourself to blend with the music, while at the same time drifting above yourself and listening to the overview. To develop your groove you have to practice the circumstances in which you want to groove, which is playing with other people.

"The spaces in the music have to groove as well as the notes—you have to be comfortable with the spaces. Many people get shaky coming back in after rests, so they play a lot of notes to plug up the holes.

> "Groove is the body language of music. It is the difference between a sequence of notes and a bass line. The groove puts butts in seats, moves feet, and fills the dance floor. It is the bassist's be-all and end-all, and the secret ingredient of a good time."
>
> —*Dave Pomeroy,*
> *Nashville session bassist, producer, and solo artist*

"You also need to develop a lighter touch on the instrument. A lot of bass players slap the strings or the bass in order to fill up the spaces, or play too hard in an attempt to keep time. That's not the same thing as using a percussive technique. You have to be able to put yourself emotionally into the music without tensing up. When the wrists and arms tighten, you lose your tone and stamina.

"When you work on your groove, you're working on music, as well. You need to know where you are in the music. If you're confident about the song, the melody and chords, it releases you and you groove well. When you have that overview of a song, you can groove better because you understand your role in the music.

"Playing without drums is a great way to strengthen your groove. When you take the drums away, you lose that statement of the beat, and it becomes your responsibility. It's also important for bass players to learn to play with just one other musician and take responsibility for the groove. That exposes if you have a good groove or not, and if you have any anxiety about the spaces in the music.

"I don't identify myself with any particular type of groove. How I play is oriented to the music I'm playing at the moment. When I practice I work on things that will get me around the instrument, but when it's game time, it becomes a matter of listening. You can't do that by yourself. It's all about listening to the music in the moment."

Chapter 5

Groove Metaphysics

One of the great aspects of being human is the potential for moments of unparalleled joy. We have all had those flashes when it seemed the pieces of a great puzzle were falling into place, each effortlessly finding its proper spot. When an action triggers a perfect reaction that sets into motion a chain of ideal events, you feel connected to the whole, an integral part of the everythingness that is life. The sense of ease that accompanies everything you do creates the feeling of floating along a beautiful river. Studied at great length, this universal experience has been called "the flow" and "the optimal experience." An optimal experience has been characterized as:

- A challenging activity that requires skill
- The merging of action and awareness
- Concentration and highly focused attention
- Lacking a sense of worry about losing control
- The loss of self-consciousness
- The transformation of time
- A sense of playfulness
- A feeling of being in control

This list accurately describes the feeling of being in the groove; in fact, groove is the musician's way of describing flow. Author Mihaly Csikszentmihalyi describes the state in his book *The Evolving Self* [Perennial].

> When challenges are high and personal skills are used to the utmost, we experience this rare state of consciousness. The first symptom of flow is a narrowing of attention on a clearly defined goal. We feel involved, concentrated, absorbed. We know what must be done, and we get immediate feedback as to how well we are doing. . . . The well-matched use of skills provides a sense of control over our actions, yet because we are too busy to think of ourselves, it does not matter whether we are in control or not, whether we are winning or losing. Often we feel a sense of transcendence, as if the boundaries of the self had been expanded. The sailor feels at one with the wind, the boat, and the sea; the singer feels a mysterious sense of universal harmony. In those moments the awareness of time disappears, and hours seem to flash by without our noticing.

When you're in the groove, your awareness of your surroundings fades into the background. All that exists is the moment, the hookup with the drums, the connection between all the musical elements. Because music is the byproduct of this connection, listeners receive this energy and, if it resonates in them, fall into the groove with you. As bassists, groove is our lifeblood. The ability to create the groove is the single most desired trait in a bass player. Many people pursue technique as a goal, but technique is merely an empty container that remains useless until there is something to fill it. Some chase externals like image, equipment, or cleverness, but these superficialities do not ensure groove. Through this book you have learned many ideas, techniques, and styles to help you groove, but the final and most important step must come from within yourself.

If we accept that all things are basically in a state of vibration—matter, light, and sound—then we can come to see that our entire existence is essentially one enormous groove. The varying vibrational frequencies that exist in a musical performance are mirrored by the different vibrations of the physical world around us. Every rock, tree, body of water, blade of grass has its own vibration. Even the most mundane aspects of your daily life are actually a groove waiting to be felt—all that need happen is for you to become receptive to the vibrations. A radio is just a box of electrical components, sitting there doing nothing—until you turn it on. So many of us are just that: potential, unplugged, only in need of an outlet and a flip of the switch. Once turned on, the radio can pick up a wide range of vibrations, and the same is true of the musician. Make yourself a receiver for the vibrations that surround you, and you will find the groove. By letting the vibrations resonate within you, you will find *your* groove. Musicians act as relay stations, picking up the groove and retransmitting it to the next relay. It is your responsibility as an individual to make yourself a "clear channel" for the groove—it must be broadcast at the same (or stronger) signal as when it was received. A weak link in the signal chain—in this case, a band—will kill the groove. If you're the weak link, no one will want to include you in the chain.

Playing music that doesn't groove is a deadening experience. You come home tired, cranky, feeling like you've been beat up. You can learn valuable lessons about what *not* to do from these experiences, but far too many players stay in these situations well beyond the point of learning anything from them. Convinced that they need the work, the money, the chance to play, many settle for less than enlivening musical experiences because they believe they have no choice. If they were to consider the negative effects of this attitude, they might try a little harder to find a groove.

The effects of stress on the body and mind are well documented. Doctors have designated stress as a primary cause of many illnesses. It's easy to see how someone locked into a dead-end job, working for a corporation they fear, managed by people they despise, making barely enough money to live on, and getting no respect might develop stress-related disorders. But what about musicians? Playing in a grooveless group can be just as debilitating to your health. As a musician, you send out energy when you play. It freely circulates within the group, and, if all the elements are in place, the groove happens and everyone is happy, energized, and in the pocket. You may send out your energy, but if it meets resistance, it ricochets back at you. You are essentially a conduit for electrical energy—it comes in one way, follows the circuit path, and goes out. If there is a break in the path, an exposed wire, you get a short circuit and start blowing fuses. After a while, the circuitbreaker may fail and that current can come slamming back at you with disastrous results. Tendinitis is only the tip of the iceberg when it comes to the damage created by groove resistance.

It only takes one person to kill the groove, and it can happen for any number of reasons. If the level of challenge is above the capabilities of one of the players, the groove will not happen. A similar situation can occur when one player's skill level is far above the others'. Maybe one of the players is in a state of physical or emotional distress. If they are too closed down to let the groove in, they will not benefit from its natural curative powers. Sometimes the mind can be the groove's worst enemy. Negative thought circulates throughout the bandstand like wildfire, burning up groove-fuel rapidly, leaving nothing behind. When someone isn't listening to the same channel as everyone else, the groove ceases to exist.

Whatever the cause, playing non-grooving music is unhealthy for the players, the listeners, and the planet. It is always possible that a situation can be turned around for the better. The first thing is to make sure *your* wiring isn't faulty. If you can honestly look at your contribution and say it's not your fault the band isn't grooving, then it becomes a matter of isolating the problem and approaching it with great sensitivity. Musicians tend to overidentify with their playing. Telling someone their groove isn't happening is sometimes wrongly interpreted as saying "you suck." People don't like to hear about their deficiencies, but if the subject is approached with respect, the discussion can have wonderful results. Most often the problem boils down to communication breakdown—open the lines of communication, and you may get the groove back. Still, there are times when it's hopeless. If you've tried everything to nurse the groove back to health and failed, move on. It's not worth any amount of money, fame, or free gear to stay in a dis-funk-tional relationship!

Ah, but what about when the groove *is* there? A full-strength groove is the most healing medicine available. Many times I've had to go to a gig feeling sick, only to come home feeling rejuvenated by the groove. The groove has the power to erase negative feeling; if you hit it, there's no way you can stay in a bad mood. All of life's problems melt away when you're in the pocket. It can bring people together. We've seen the power of the groove on an audience, thousands of people sharing the groove and for that moment becoming one. Within a group, the groove is the life force that makes everything happen. Bands struggle through hard times and adversity, trying to make their mark on the world, based on a belief in the power of their groove. On a much larger scale, hitting the groove sends "good vibrations" out into the universe. When you consider the high levels of bad vibrations present in our world, you can see how important it is to do your part for the planet and humanity by making the groove happen.

Opening yourself to the power of the groove, you act as a channel for perfectly aligned vibrational frequencies. When you lock in to the groove, you transmit this energy to the other members of the band, who in turn amplify the power and broadcast it to the world. Even if there is no one around to hear it, this infusion of positive energy makes a big difference. If there is an audience, then the effects of the groove get amplified to even greater levels. As a bassist, your role in the groove is unique. You are the grounding force that keeps it all together. You are a lightning rod, attracting powerful electrical forces to yourself and then acting as a conductor, harnessing these energies and sending them deep into the ground. The deeper you become rooted, the heavier the groove. While your roots may go deep, you must remain flexible up top, like a willow tree that bends with the breeze. Being too rigid above ground will cause resistance—eventually something has to break.

Music is an organic form that is reflected in the natural world that surrounds you. Everything you can perceive is vibrating particles creating patterns, some dense like a rock, some intangible like radio waves. Groove is a form of vibration that exists in an ethereal plane. You can't see it, you can't touch or taste it, but you know when it is there. It is the musician's role to mobilize this energy and amplify it for the good of the planet. Throughout time, musicians have been held in high esteem as the masters of this life force now known as groove, and as a bass player, you understand how crucial your part is in the process of nurturing, protecting, and broadcasting the groove. Next time you play, consider this: It's not just a gig, it's a sacred duty you have been entrusted with. To groove is to align yourself with the most powerful forces in the universe for the good of all. If you acknowledge this, you will find your groove can go much deeper than you ever imagined possible.

On the CD

Chapter 1

Track 1 **Anatomy of a Drum Beat:** Drum Examples 1–6

Chapter 2

Track 2 **Groove Concept and Development:** Vox Examples 1–3
Track 3 **Groove Concept and Development:** Vox Examples 4–5
Track 4 **Groove Concept and Development:** Vox Examples 6–8
Track 5 **Groove Concept and Development:** Vox Examples 9–11
Track 6 **On the *One*:** OTO Examples 1–4
Track 7 **Off da Hook:** Offbeat Examples 1–5
Track 8 **Off da Hook, Hip-Hop Style:** Swunk Examples 1–5
Track 9 **Funkin' Metronome:** Slap Examples 1–7
Track 10 **The Groove-Yard Shift:** Shift Examples 1–3
Track 11 **The Fat Factor:** Fat Examples 1–7

Chapter 3

Track 12 **The Tramp Groove:** Tramp Examples 1–7
Track 13 **The Singer-Songwriter Groove:** Singer Examples 1–6
Track 14 **The Slow 12/8 Feel:** 12/8 Examples 3–4
Track 15 **The Flat Tire Groove:** Flat Ex. 2
Track 16 **The Shuffle:** Shuffle Examples 2–5
Track 17 **The Anticipated Backbeat:** AB Examples 3–6
Track 18 **The James Brown Groove:** JB Examples 2–4
Track 19 **The Bo Diddley Beat:** Bo Examples 2–5
Track 20 **Rockin' Rhumba:** Rhumba Examples 1–9
Track 21 **The Fats Domino 12/8 Groove:** Fats Examples 1–3
Track 22 **Slow Blues:** Slow Ex. 2
Track 23 **Pumpin' Eighths:** Pumpin' Examples 1–7
Track 24 **The Twist:** Twist Examples 1–6
Track 25 **The Motown Beat:** Motown Examples 2–5
Track 26 **Rock Steady:** Rock Steady Examples 1–3
Track 27 **The Disco Octave Lick:** Disco Examples 2–4
Track 28 **Bom Bom:** Bom Bom Examples 1–5
Track 29 **The Meters—New Orleans Funk:** Meters Examples 1–3
Track 30 **Soca:** Soca Examples 1–5
Track 31 **The Jimmy Reed Groove:** Reed Examples 2–5
Track 32 **Vinny-Boom-Batz:** Vinny Examples 2–5
Track 33 **The "Green Onions" Groove:** Onions Examples 1–5
Track 34 **Cajun:** Cajun Examples 1–4
Track 35 **Zydeco:** Zydeco Examples 1–3
Track 36 **Go-Go:** Go-Go Examples 1–6

Acknowledgments

Special thanks to Dawn Friedland for her unconditional love and support through the many ordeals of the writing process. To Aimee, LeeEllen, Sonia, and Irving Friedland, and David Taylor for being family.

I'd like to thank Richard Johnston at Backbeat Books for envisioning this book as a valuable title, and for all the years he corrected my punctuation as editor of *Bass Player* magazine. Thanks to Bill Leigh, my current BP editor, for getting behind the Groove of the Month Club concept that has driven my column The Right Foot for the last two years. The column served as the source for the chapters in this book. Thanks to Jim Roberts for seeing my potential as a writer early on and giving me the opportunity to contribute to *Bass Player*. Thanks to Karl Coryat and Greg Olwell for all their help and for keeping things moving. For the book, thanks to Greg Isola for his expert proofreading and to Amy Miller for putting it all together.

Thanks to Carvin Guitars for the great tools to play, Bergantino Audio for making the best bass cabs in the world, LaBella Strings for my lifelines, and Fishman Transducers for making acoustic amplification a satisfying experience (and for the Platinum preamp).

Photo Credits

Page 99: Photo by Steve Barr
Page 100: Photo by Neil Zlozower
Page 102: Courtesy of Gary Grainger

About the Author

Bassist and educator Ed Friedland has written scores of instructional articles as a columnist and Contributing Editor for *Bass Player* magazine, and he is the author of several books, including Backbeat's *The Working Bassist's Tool Kit* and Hal Leonard's *Building Walking Bass Lines*, *Jazz Bass*, *Reggae Bass*, and *Building Rock Bass Lines*. His DVD, *Slap Bass: The Ultimate Guide*, is also available from Hal Leonard.

Ed has performed with numerous artists in the jazz, pop, and classical worlds, including Robben Ford, Bud Shank, Larry Coryell, Paul Horn, Michal Urbaniak, the Drifters, the Marvelettes, Fabian, the Opera Company of Boston, and the Tucson Symphony Orchestra. His theater credits include *Little Shop of Horrors* (Boston and Tokyo), *Nite Club Confidential*, *A Closer Walk with Patsy Cline*, and *42nd St.* A resident of Tucson, Arizona, Ed has taught at Arizona State University as well as Berklee College of Music and Boston College. He continues to do clinics around the United States. You can find information about all things bass at his Web site, www.edfriedland.com.